INDIA INC'S
GREATEST
TURNAROUNDS

INDIA INC'S GREATEST TURNAROUNDS

CEOs of JSW Steel, Tata Steel, L&T,
Raymond, and Religare Enterprises
Share Their Financial Success Stories

DEV CHATTERJEE
WITH PRAGYA CHATTERJEE

JAICO PUBLISHING HOUSE

Ahmedabad Bangalore Chennai
Delhi Hyderabad Kolkata Mumbai

Published by Jaico Publishing House
A-2 Jash Chambers, 7-A Sir Phirozshah Mehta Road
Fort, Mumbai - 400 001
jaicopub@jaicobooks.com
www.jaicobooks.com

INDIA INC'S GREATEST TURNAROUNDS
ISBN 978-93-49358-13-3

First Jaico Impression: 2025

Page design and layout by Inosoft Systems, Delhi

Printed by
Nutech Print Services - India, New Delhi

CONTENTS

FOREWORD

India Inc's Greatest Turnarounds seems to have genesis in a stark yet undeniable reality: failure is not the end, but rather a stepping stone towards redemption. Across India, numerous companies have transcended failure, crafting remarkable comebacks that not only revived their fortunes but also extended a lifeline to others in distress. Tales of adversity and resurgence intertwine to form a narrative of remarkable turnarounds, with lessons and inspiration. This book delves deep into the heart of these narratives, exploring the intricacies of financial and economic distress, strategic repositioning, and visionary leadership that drove companies from the precipice of collapse to the pinnacle of success. Through meticulous research and insightful analysis, this book illuminates the trajectory undertaken by iconic companies in their quest for rejuvenation.

In my professional journey, I have intimately encountered the tapestry of failure and redemption. Here, I endeavour to present my take on the incidence of failure, elucidating the concerns it spawns and the mechanisms in place to prevent and salvage it. In the grand tapestry of commerce we created artificial persons, namely, companies, to carry on our legacy forever. The company structure matured with time, acquiring attractive and powerful properties like separate legal personality, perpetual existence, and limited liability. These attributes offered significant advantages over other organisational structures, making companies the preferred business vehicle. The provision of economic freedom gave a fillip to organized economic activity. With the withdrawal of restrictions on size, businesses exploited economies of scale and scope. These promoted the exponential growth of companies, many of them growing larger, some of them beyond borders, with time.

In the contemporary landscape, companies have become an integral part of our daily existence, permeating every aspect of our lives. It is difficult to imagine life without them. They house, feed, clothe, and employ us. Moreover, they are custodians of the economy's resources, creating wealth and sharing the same among stakeholders. As growth engines, they hold the hope of prosperity for posterity. They often have organisational capital over and above their tangible assets. The closure of a company not only extinguishes this hope but also erodes organisational capital accumulated over time. It takes years of effort to bring up a company which can replace an existing one. The premature demise of many companies has the potential to precipitate economic destabilisation. Recognising their pivotal role in sustaining societal well-being and economic prosperity, several institutions have emerged to safeguard their lives.

Till a century ago, companies had lifespans that surpassed those of humans. Kongo Gumi Co. Ltd., a Japanese company revered for its temple construction expertise, succumbed to debt in 2006 after living a record 1429 years. There are a few thousand-year-old companies still around. They are rare surviving gems of a bygone era. A McKinsey & Co. study revealed a stark decline in the longevity of S&P 500 companies, plummeting from an average of 90 years in 1935 to a mere 18 years by 2016. Recent studies indicate that the average life of a publicly traded company, considering acquisitions, mergers, and bankruptcy, is about 10 years. The life of a company is more in danger today than ever before, despite the presence of institutional safeguards.

The life of a company has three enemies. The first is the enemy within, namely, internal discord among the stakeholders. A company is an amalgam of many stakeholders. Each stakeholder has a unique objective function, with a distinct set of rights, interests, and levels of engagement with the company. Consequently, conflicting agendas often arise, pitting stakeholders against one another and, at times, against the company's interests. This discord is exacerbated by the transient nature of modern shareholders, many of whom hold shares of the company for a fraction of a second, some of them abandoning ship at the faintest hint of trouble. The departure of a significant shareholder may orphan the company, begging the question: whose company is it anyway? In their drive to maximise their upside while enjoying limited liability, shareholders may inadvertently expose the company/ society to unlimited liabilities. Examples are the Bhopal gas tragedy and the Satyam fiasco. A disruption in the delicate balance between the limited liability and the unlimited liability jeopardises the life of the company.

The state has instituted a comprehensive framework of institutional norms, collectively known as corporate governance, to safeguard the well-being of companies. These norms encompass a spectrum of measures, including the appointment of independent directors, oversight of key managerial personnel, regulation of related-party transactions, protection of minority interests, financial and secretarial audits, and the timely disclosure of material information. Additionally, corporate governance extends to matters of taxation, subsidies, and corporate social responsibility, ensuring that companies operate in alignment with broader societal interests. While these standards aim to harmonise and reconcile the diverse interests of stakeholders, some companies surpass the mandated norms, proactively adopting aspirational governance practices to fortify their resilience against existential threats.

The second and the fiercest is the enemy from outside, namely, the market. Every other company in the market is its predator: a company swallows another for its growth, through hostile or friendly takeover. Further, it is state policy to promote competition and innovation in the marketplace to drive growth. An efficient firm kills inefficient ones in competition. A company loses life when it fails to compete with its peers in the same business for reasons such as poor organisation, inefficient management, and even malfeasance. Moreover, the relentless march of innovation continually reshapes market dynamics, rendering established business models obsolete. This phenomenon, known as creative destruction, often destroys more companies than it creates! Additionally, external factors beyond a company's control, such as shifts in policy, resource depletion, market access restrictions, geopolitical conflicts, natural disasters, or unprecedented events like the Covid-19 pandemic can precipitate its downfall.

For a company to thrive in the long term, it must navigate the twin challenges of competition and innovation with finesse. If it lives too much in the present to survive competition, it may disregard innovation essential for long-term viability. Conversely, if it lives too much in the future to survive innovation, it may ignore competition essential for existence. Hence, maintaining the balance between the present and the future is imperative. Moreover, prudent risk management is essential; excessive risk-taking in the pursuit of survival can cut short its life. Strategies such as resilience building, adaptive measures, robust research and development initiatives, sustainable business models, visionary leadership, and readiness for unforeseen contingencies are indispensable in mitigating risks and ensuring longevity. However, it is entirely for the stakeholders to build the muscle of the company to withstand the onslaught of competition and innovation.

The third enemy is unfair battles in the marketplace. A company may not survive in a market where a dominant company resorts to unfair pricing; if its cost of capital is high as compared to another company that manipulates the market for its securities; if it dutifully pays corporate tax while another in the same business dodges taxes; if it fails to enforce contracts against other parties because of weak institutions, etc. The rule of law shields such law-abiding companies/ businesses from unfair battles. Its effectiveness, however, depends on the quality of laws (for competition, securities, taxation, contracts, etc.) and the state machinery administering these laws.

Hence, a company may get into stress/ fail if it lacks robust corporate governance, if it fails to navigate the landscape of competition and innovation, or the state fails to shield it from unfair market practices. Recognising these threats, the Indian state has proactively established institutional frameworks to facilitate corporate rescue and revival. From corporate debt restructuring to insolvency resolution frameworks, stakeholders are armed with a diverse toolkit to chart a course towards sustainable recovery.

Furthermore, these frameworks introduce new stakeholders if existing ones falter in their duties. They empower the board of directors, responsible for appointing and overseeing executive management, to replace it in case of failure, as outlined in contractual agreements. Additionally, shareholders, vested with the authority to elect directors to the board and monitor their performance, may replace them under the provisions of the Companies Act, 2013, should they prove ineffective. Moreover, a promising cohort of shareholders may even supplant the incumbent set in the dynamic realm of corporate control. Notably, the Insolvency and Bankruptcy Code, 2016 (Code) brings in creditors to rescue the company when shareholders have failed to guard its life.

The Code has emerged as a beacon of hope for failing companies. This enables creditors to rescue a company through a resolution plan. It confers extraordinary powers on them for this purpose: (a) they may seek the best resolution plan from the global market, in a significant departure from previous mechanisms that confined resolutions from existing promoters; (b) they may take and/ or cause a haircut of any amount to any or all stakeholders as may be required for rescuing the company; and (c) the resolution plan may entail any measure(s)—a change of management, technology, or product portfolio; acquisition or disposal of assets, businesses, or undertakings; restructuring of organisation, business model, ownership, or balance sheet; strategies of turn-around, buy-out, merger, amalgamation, acquisition, or takeover; etc. Yet, some companies may be beyond repair and have to be closed. The Code facilitates the orderly liquidation of such companies.

Despite their apparent 'immortality', it is not uncommon for companies to face periods of adversity. However, proactive measures can prevent, postpone, reduce, or altogether avoid such stress. It is also possible to rescue a company from the brink of failure. It is not good either for the company or the economy to keep a company under stress for long, which only destroys value and heightens the risk of closure. It is also not good to stigmatise an honest business failure as it discourages entrepreneurial risk-taking. In such cases, entrepreneurs and management must acknowledge the reality and, if necessary, gracefully step aside, allowing others with the capability to salvage the failing enterprise.

Despite these interventions, not all companies bounce back. However, those that do, provide invaluable lessons for business leaders, policymakers, and aspiring entrepreneurs alike. The saga of JSW Steel, Tata Steel, L&T, Raymond, and Religare Enterprises, as illuminated in this book, serves as a testament to the indomitable spirit of Indian entrepreneurship. Each chapter unveils the strategic manoeuvres, innovative tactics, and unwavering resolve that propelled these companies toward unprecedented success.

India Inc's Greatest Turnarounds isn't merely a compendium of past triumphs; it's a manifesto of hope and possibility. It celebrates the unyielding spirit of innovation and the enduring legacy of those who defied conventional wisdom. As readers embark on this voyage of exploration, may these stories kindle a flame of inspiration, urging companies to embrace change, navigate challenges, and emerge stronger in the crucible of adversity.

Dr. M. S. Sahoo

Former Distinguished Professor, National Law University, Delhi and Former Chairperson, Insolvency and Bankruptcy Board of India

AUTHORS' NOTE

In India, entrepreneurs are often celebrated for their success in business publications, but it's crucial to acknowledge the arduous journey beneath the surface. While there are numerous success stories, many entrepreneurs struggle with Indian bureaucracy, high interest rates, and unexpected policy changes—all of which could cause failure despite the best planning and efforts.

In a previous book, *The Meltdown—India Inc's Biggest Implosions* (Rupa Publications, 2020), the authors examined the failure of some of India's top companies and the reasons behind their bankruptcies.

In this book, we delve into the essence of entrepreneurship within India's dynamic and occasionally unpredictable business environment. What factors enabled certain companies to thrive despite significant challenges? Was it the leadership, the quality of their teams, their networking skills or some other elements?

Entrepreneurs are crucial for driving innovation in the world, for creating jobs, and fostering economic growth and prosperity. It is imperative, therefore, that all stakeholders provide support to companies during challenging times. CEOs often emphasize in interviews that timely support from stakeholders, including banks and regulators, can help preserve a company's value.

The success of an enterprise is not merely a product of luck or circumstance; it is the culmination of decades of relentless hard work, determination, and resilience. The stories shared in these pages highlight that failure is not a full stop but a stepping stone to success.

Consider billionaire Sajjan Jindal's project in Vijayanagar, Karnataka, which introduced Corex technology for the first time in India to produce steel. The project faced a significant setback on its first day due to unseasonal rains. Undeterred, Jindal persevered, becoming an inspiration for other Indian entrepreneurs.

Similarly, Tata Steel has turned around several loss-making businesses including Neelachal Ispat Nigam acquired from the government and Bhushan Steel acquired in an auction of distressed assets by the lenders. With the support of an experienced team, Tata Steel, led by its Managing Director TV Narendran, revived these plants in record time.

The entrepreneurs featured in this book have faced numerous unseen circumstances and powerful adversaries, with their efforts often seeming destined to falter. But they fought back. Our research shows that most companies, given the opportunity by their lenders and the regulators, can bounce back quite fast.

While some companies—like Gautam Hari Singhania's fashion retailer, Raymond—nearly shut down due to the Covid-19 pandemic, others like Larsen & Toubro, led by its former Chairman Anil Manibhai Naik, faced powerful conglomerates in a takeover battle. You will read about how both companies overcame these challenges where several others would have folded, mainly because of their leaders' convictions, and the support they were able to garner.

Despite his humble origins, Anil Manibhai Naik played a remarkable role in creating the mega-conglomerate that L&T is today, with a market valuation of ₹5 trillion. Naik's contribution to reinventing L&T is the stuff of corporate legends. His approach to stopping the takeover bid in its tracks was unique and is a lesson in ingenuity for young entrepreneurs.

Meanwhile, Gautam Singhania steered Raymond through the rough waters of the pandemic lockdowns, to help the company emerge stronger than ever before. The measures that Singhania and his team took to streamline the company—improving its efficiency and enhancing accountability—have led to a post-pandemic resurgence of Raymond.

In their interviews with us, entrepreneurs discussed the hardships they faced and the strategies they used to turn around their companies. Their success stories have the power to inspire the next generation of entrepreneurs in India. We wanted to share their narratives so that every CEO or budding leader gets an idea about their template for success.

Each chapter in this book is a beacon of hope for entrepreneurs facing tough times, and a lesson for aspiring businessmen to keep fighting, just as the leaders featured here did.

Rashmi Saluja, Executive Chairperson of Religare Enterprises, is spotlighted in the book for several reasons. Saluja took on the billionaire Burman family, owners of Dabur India, for control of Religare. The Delhi-based financial services company nearly shut down after its former promoters were accused of financial shenanigans. Saluja's networking skills across the spectrum of business, regulators and politics was the main reason for Religare's turnaround. Read on about the outcome of this battle between Saluja and the Burmans, for more insights.

After our interviews with numerous CEOs, we've concluded that India must stop prosecuting commercial failures and punishing entrepreneurs.

This book serves as a testament to the resilience, ingenuity, and unwavering spirit of Indian entrepreneurs. It is also a call to action for banks and financial institutions to recognize the potential within these individuals and to actively support them, understanding that their success benefits not just the entrepreneur but the entire community and its economy.

Data reveals that even some of India's top conglomerates, including the Tatas (in wireless telephony services), and the Aditya Birla Group (in online fashion retailing), have failed in some ventures. The role of an entrepreneur is to take risks, which may lead either to success or to utter failure. However, punishing these pioneers is not the solution. To quote Steve Jobs, "If you're afraid of failing, you won't get very far."

Entrepreneurs who have diligently repaid banks until economic or sectoral downturns should not be viewed with suspicion. Unfortunately, the punishment for failed entrepreneurs in India is quite harsh. To promote the next generation of entrepreneurs, India must soften its draconian laws.

Ease of doing business in India as compared to that in other nations is still a long way off desired levels. Leaders of India Inc. complain about the high-handedness of investigating agencies, which diminishes their enthusiasm for taking risks. Trials on companies can drag on for years, and entrepreneurs suffer in silence amid unfair social stigma.

For instance, between 2014 and 2024, numerous cases were filed against business people by the Central Bureau of Investigation and the Enforcement Directorate. The data, however, shows poor conviction rates. Even in the infamous 2G spectrum allotment cases, which damaged India's business environment between 2008 and 2014, the trial court did not convict a single business owner.

Debt restructuring schemes are another cause of concern for entrepreneurs. Sometimes the Asset Reconstruction Companies (ARCs) buy loans from banks at 10 cents to a dollar, but they squeeze the companies hard to get their own money back with high returns. The ARC model needs a relook if entrepreneurship is to be encouraged in India. In the current model, both banks and promoters suffer as ARCs take the largest share of the pie.

For businesses to thrive and for India to become a developed nation that creates jobs for the next generation, we have to ease laws that impede the growth of entrepreneurship. Together, let us champion the cause of Indian entrepreneurs, recognizing that with the right support from the government and other stakeholders, many more will succeed.

INTRODUCTION

A TALE OF TWO COMPANIES

Manoj Tirodkar is a quintessential Mumbaikar. Hailing from a middle-class Maharashtrian family in Konkan, Tirodkar exemplifies the typical rags to riches story seen in India's financial capital. Starting his business journey at the age of 17, Tirodkar's ascent into the Indian corporate world was propelled by unwavering determination, tireless labour, and indomitable grit.

In 1987, Tirodkar embarked on his entrepreneurial venture by founding GTL Limited, a pioneering network services firm that strategically positioned itself to capitalize India's burgeoning digitization wave.

With the liberalization of India's wireless telephony sector, several well-established giants right from the Tatas and Birlas to the Ruias and Ambanis rushed into the rapidly expanding market. The new mobile phone companies required a robust telecom tower infrastructure, creating a ripe opportunity that Tirodkar seized upon. He diversified into telecom towers and established a new company—GTL Infrastructure (GTL Infra) in 2005-06.

Recognizing the inefficiency of each telecom provider erecting their own towers, GTL Infra emerged as a rare independent entity capable of servicing all telecom operators seamlessly.

Recognizing the inefficiency of each telecom provider erecting their own towers, GTL Infra emerged as a rare independent entity capable of servicing all telecom operators seamlessly. To fund the new enterprise, GTL group sold India's first homegrown unicorn (company with a valuation of $1 billion or more) to top international investors including Morgan Stanley, GE Capital, Alliance Capital, and four others in 1998-99. The proceeds were used to grow GTL's business in India.

In a stunning move in 2010, Tirodkar acquired wireless telephone service provider Aircel's 17,500 telecom towers for a staggering ₹8,400 crore, marking one of the era's most significant M&A (mergers and acquisitions) transactions. Aircel, under the ownership of Malaysia's Maxis, wanted to reduce its debt burden—so it offloaded its towers nationwide to GTL Infra, cementing a lucrative alliance by guaranteeing business through tower rentals. Aircel also contracted an additional 20,000 future tenancies over three years from 2010 to 2013.

With numerous telecom firms vying to deliver wireless telephony services to consumers in every nook and corner of the country, telecom towers became a prized commodity. GTL Infra found itself perfectly poised to meet the escalating demand.

The telecom landscape underwent a seismic shift in 2012 when the Supreme Court, following the controversial "2G scam", cancelled all licences granted in 2008 by the Manmohan Singh-led government.

But the telecom landscape underwent a seismic shift in 2012 when the Supreme Court, following the controversial "2G scam", cancelled all licences granted in 2008 by the Manmohan Singh-led government. The SC said the government should auction spectrum (radio waves) to telecom companies instead of allotting them.

Overnight, the SC order led to the dissolution of several mobile phone companies including Videocon, Unitech, Sistema, and Swan Telecom among others.

Within a few years, Aircel—grappling with the challenge posed by Reliance Jio's free services—succumbed to financial turmoil and ultimately ceased operations in 2018. GTL Infra, whose business model hinged on the anticipated meteoric growth of the telecom sector, found itself confronted with an abrupt and unforgiving reality. Being their largest customer, Aircel owed ₹13,000 crore in unpaid future rentals to GTL Infrastructure.

As the telecom sector's fortunes plunged, both GTL and its subsidiary, GTL Infra, sought Corporate Debt Restructuring (CDR) from banks, a lifeline extended in recognition of the telecom sector's plight. In 2011, GTL Infra's lenders opted for CDR as the path forward. Over the restructuring period between 2011 and 2016, the company repaid a substantial ₹6,469 crore to the banks. However, persistent adverse conditions in the telecom industry, epitomized by the Supreme Court's cancellation of 122 telecom licenses in 2012, rendered a significant portion of its debt unsustainable.

In September 2016, the banks implemented a Strategic Debt Restructuring (SDR) scheme for the company, converting approximately ₹4,500 crore of the company's debt into equity. Post-conversion, lenders held a commanding 63.16 per cent stake in the company and commenced the search for new investors, all while enduring significant tenancy losses amid client bankruptcies and closures.

Ultimately, however, the pursuit of a new buyer for their stake proved futile, as between 2016 and 2017, Aircel, RCom,

Sistema Shyam, Tata Teleservices, and Telenor closed shop. In July 2018, the Union Bank of India proposed the sale of GTL Infra's debt to a consortium led by Edelweiss Asset Reconstruction Company. The Union Bank noted that while GTL Infra had diligently serviced its financial obligations under the SDR, it still had to sell the debt to adhere to the Reserve Bank of India's Revised Framework for Resolution of Stressed Assets. This effectively dissolved the existing debt resolution schemes.

Despite truncated operations, GTL Infra managed to repay over ₹19,000 crore to its lenders since the fiscal year (FY) 2010-11 until March 2024, a feat that stood in stark contrast to its staggering losses exceeding ₹17,000 crore. These losses were, of course, triggered by the spate of telecom operator closures following the 2G licence cancellations.

While most of GTL's lenders adhered to the consortium's decision to transfer debt to Edelweiss Asset Reconstruction Company, one of its lenders—Canara Bank—moved the National Company Law Tribunal (NCLT) for debt resolution under the Insolvency and Bankruptcy Code, 2016. But the Mumbai bench of the NCLT dismissed Canara Bank's petition, deeming both companies as "going concerns" that faithfully repaid their debts.

The NCLT's verdict underscored GTL Infra's robust financial standing, with monthly revenues of ₹130 crore (net of tax) indicating its viability as a "going concern".

The company's debt repayment track record further exemplified its ability to manage sustainable debt.

GTL Infra also pursued claims against Aircel entities, securing directives from the NCLT which asked the defaulters to pay ₹900 crore to the company. The court said that GTL Infra had to recover ₹49.84 crore from Tata Teleservices, ₹20.38 crore from American Tower Corporation, and ₹351 crore from the government-owned BSNL, offering a substantial pool of resources to service residual debt.

The NCLT's comprehensive assessment affirmed GTL Infra's sustained viability under its current management. It emphasized the company's sound financial health, dismissing the request for bankruptcy proceedings.

Notably, the court said that GTL Infra's extensive claims against clients far exceeded Canara Bank's bankruptcy petition.

Following the NCLT's ruling, the Insolvency and Bankruptcy Board of India (IBBI)—an Indian government body overseeing bankruptcies—and Canara Bank filed an appeal at the National Company Law Appellate Tribunal (NCLAT), New Delhi. The NCLAT, on February 7, 2023, dismissed the IBBI's petition as infructuous on grounds of maintainability. However, as of October 25, 2024, the NCLAT has, while allowing Canara Bank's appeal, set aside NCLT's order and remanded the case to NCLT for a fresh hearing.

As of October 25, 2024, the NCLAT has, while allowing Canara Bank's appeal, set aside NCLT's order and remanded the case to NCLT for a fresh hearing.

During this tumultuous period, lenders sold GTL Infra's loan to Edelweiss Asset Reconstruction Company, fetching an additional ₹1,900 crore. GTL Infra staunchly maintained its non-default status, having diligently adhered to the debt restructuring scheme sanctioned by bank boards. GTL Infra is still operating but with truncated operations, even as litigation goes on and on.

In summary, GTL Infra and its promoter have consistently demonstrated unwavering commitment and resilience by fulfilling debt obligations despite severe external adversities. Remarkably, this has been achieved without raising new capital or resorting to incremental borrowings since 2011, while simultaneously ensuring operational stability and business sustainability.

Essar Steel was an entity entwined with the dynamic journey of the billionaire Ruia brothers, Shashi and Ravi. The Ruia duo set out on their business operations in the late 1960s, launching a modest shipping enterprise in

Chennai. They astutely seized the early waves of economic liberalization initiated by the then Finance Minister—Dr. Manmohan Singh—in 1991, a period when virtually every business they founded turned into gold.

Through the 1990s, the Ruias solidified their presence in the industrial landscape by establishing a world-class oil refinery in Jamnagar, a state-of-the-art steel plant in Hazira near Surat, and foraying into capital-intensive sectors like wireless telephony in India. Notably, they discerned a burgeoning opportunity in the realm of Business Process Outsourcing, leading to their acquisition in the early 2000s of Aegis, a BPO firm that catered to marquee clients worldwide.

The Ruia brothers, in collaboration with their sons Prashant and Anshuman, expanded their horizons by venturing into overseas assets. Their international diversification began with the acquisition of Algoma Steel (Canada) and Minnesota Steel (USA) in 2007. In 2011, the Ruias acquired Shell's Stanlow oil refinery in Europe for a substantial sum of $350 million, providing them a strategic foothold in creating a global oil trading platform. Their early investments in India's wireless telephony sector culminated in a significant 33 per cent stake in Vodafone Essar.

But it was Essar Steel which, despite several fund infusions by the promoters, and debts recast by lenders, started

It was Essar Steel which, despite several fund infusions by the promoters, and debts recast by lenders, started defaulting on loans by 2017.

defaulting on loans by 2017. To generate capital, the group had earlier initiated a worldwide asset sale. One notable transaction included the sale of their 33 per cent stake in Vodafone India to the British behemoth, Vodafone Group PLC, for a colossal $5 billion in 2011. This windfall not only alleviated overseas banking debts, but also marked a significant financial achievement for Essar Group.

However, these sales of assets were not enough. By June 2017, the company found itself among the biggest defaulters in India. This happened when the Reserve Bank of India (RBI) asked banks to refer the top 12 defaulters to the National Company Law Tribunal for debt resolution under the Modi government's new law—Insolvency and Bankruptcy Code of 2016 (IBC).

The IBC aimed to resolve bank debt by selling assets of insolvent companies to the highest bidder, and removing the old management of the company.

Several formidable external factors had impacted operations of the steel company. The Ruias had invested a staggering ₹50,000 crore in their world-class integrated steel plant in Hazira, Surat, boasting a production capacity of 10 million tonnes annually. However, this ambitious facility was geographically distant from its raw material sources in Odisha, Chhattisgarh, and Jharkhand in Eastern India, although crucially situated to serve its customer base in the western region.

Essar Steel had strategically established the gas-based Hazira steel plant on the west coast of India, bolstered by assurances from the Indian government regarding continued gas supply. Nevertheless, the company's operations and financial viability took a severe hit when oil and gas producer Reliance Industries' gas field off the Andhra Pradesh coast encountered difficulties.

> Essar Steel's operations and financial viability took a severe hit when oil and gas producer Reliance Industries' gas field off the Andhra Pradesh coast encountered difficulties.

From 1990 to 2010, the Indian government had accorded top priority to the steel sector, furnishing Essar Steel with natural gas on a priority basis to aid the nation's infrastructure development. This favourable gas supply arrangement persisted even after a gas policy shift in 2005. In fact, in 2009, the Empowered Group of Ministers had directed the prioritized supply of natural gas to the Essar Steel plant, ensuring that its operational needs were met.

However, as gas supplies faltered, the Indian government under the leadership of Dr. Manmohan Singh reclassified the steel sector from a "priority sector" to a "non-core area" in March 2011. Consequently, Reliance Industries, the gas producer in the Krishna Godavari basin, was directed to curtail its gas supply to Essar Steel in the event of a shortage.

Despite the government's earlier assurance to Essar Steel on steady gas allocation, its supply was abruptly stopped in July 2011. The steel plant was forced to curtail production, setting off a cascade of adverse consequences.

Despite the government's earlier assurance to Essar Steel on steady gas allocation, its supply was abruptly stopped in July 2011.

Between 2011 and 2016, Essar Steel incurred staggering losses of approximately ₹26,000 crore due to the Indian government's decision to terminate its gas supply. Thereafter, the company began defaulting on its bank loans.

During their negotiations with lenders for debt restructuring, the Ruias offered various solutions to inject additional cash as equity infusion by inviting private equity funds. They also extended an offer to reduce their ownership stake in the company from 100 per cent to below 40 per cent, while converting their lenders' debt into a 34 per cent stake.

The Ruias said that the proposed sale of a stake to the American hedge fund Farallon Capital would be their second major asset sale. This was set to follow the momentous $13 billion sale of their entire stake in Essar Oil, a Jamnagar based refinery, to Russian oil giant Rosneft in 2017. With Rosneft assuming control of Essar Oil's loans, the Ruias asserted that these debts were no longer a liability on the group's balance sheet.

But Essar Steel's proposal was rejected by the banks, prompting the State Bank of India to refer the company to the bankruptcy court in June 2017, to comply with the RBI's directive. The steel plant was eventually acquired by the world's largest steel firm, ArcelorMittal, as a joint venture with Nippon Steel, following a highly litigated auction process.

∞

The tales of Manoj Tirodkar and the Ruia brothers shed light on the formidable challenges faced by Indian entrepreneurs as they navigate the complex business landscape of India. India's corporate history is replete with instances where the nation celebrates success but demonstrates a low tolerance for failure. Entrepreneurs like Tirodkar and the Ruias, who grappled with the daunting task of resuscitating their companies, are not alone in their struggles.

Of course, some Indian companies such as JSW Steel have managed to rebound from financial adversity thanks to a robust steel cycle and a consistent supply of raw materials. And as we've seen earlier, GTL Infra is still alive and kicking, despite being weighed down by lawsuits. The case of Essar Steel serves as a stark contrast, as it couldn't cope with the abrupt cessation of its energy supply, and had to be sold.

Across the globe, governments often extend a helping hand to local companies by offering subsidies or low cost raw materials to mitigate challenging circumstances. A case in point is Tata Steel UK, which received a substantial £500 million aid package from the British government. This funding was to help the Tata company shift to an environmentally friendly electric furnace and reduce its reliance on coal. With this subsidy in tow, Tata Steel UK is poised to channel additional investments into the British steel making plant, ultimately creating jobs in the Port Talbot region, 286 kilometres west of London.

As India ascends the global economic ranks, it is imperative to scrutinize the myriad challenges confronting Indian entrepreneurs. Adverse court rulings, disruptions in the raw materials supply chain, and natural disasters can wreak havoc on companies that are integral to the nation's economic machinery. Often, protracted legal battles not only drain a company's resources but also impose a penalizing burden on entrepreneurs, discouraging them from taking risks.

Often, protracted legal battles not only drain a company's resources but also impose a penalizing burden on entrepreneurs, discouraging them from taking risks.

In response to these challenges, some Indian entrepreneurs have opted to redirect their investments overseas. A compelling example is that of the Ruia brothers, who are investing $4.5 billion in a new steel plant in Saudi Arabia, and towards energy transition in the United Kingdom. The adverse business conditions prevailing in India play a pivotal role in driving this trend.

While addressing a Nasscom event in February 2017, Mukesh Ambani—India's most successful businessman and Chair of Reliance Industries—shared a vital insight: that business failures are a normal part of the entrepreneurial journey. Ambani candidly acknowledged his own previous failures before attaining success. His invaluable advice, "Never get disheartened by failures. Learn from them, but never give up," serves as a timeless lesson for all future entrepreneurs.

HISTORY OF CORPORATE DEBT RESTRUCTURING IN INDIA

Bad loans have been a perennial problem for the Indian banking and corporate sectors over the past few decades. High debt has crippled several companies and affected the balance sheets of their lenders. In response, lenders initiated various schemes to assist companies facing difficulties.

In 2016, Indian Prime Minister Narendra Modi and the late Finance Minister Arun Jaitley introduced a new bankruptcy law—the Insolvency and Bankruptcy Code (IBC)—intended to help banks recover part of their dues.

The new law aimed to expedite recovery for banks while being fair to all stakeholders, including the employees of ailing companies, their creditors, and their suppliers. The IBC was designed to tip the scales in favour of banks—it allowed banks to sack the board of directors of defaulting companies and to appoint an independent auditor to oversee the auction to the highest bidder.

On an average, banks recovered around 33 per cent of their dues, while the rest was considered a haircut—the amount banks forgo to settle an account.

The objective of the Modi government to help Indian banks recover their dues has largely been met by the new law. As a result, banks' balance sheets now look healthier as compared to when the law was enacted.

Interestingly, the IBC was not India's first attempt to solve the bad debt problem. In the past, the Indian government and the Reserve Bank of India had taken several steps to reduce bad loans. The first such framework was introduced by the union government in 1985 with the enactment of the Sick Industrial Companies (Special Provisions) Act (SICA). This law was aimed at timely detection of sick industrial units and taking speedy action to resolve the financial crisis through a board of experts—the Board for Industrial and Financial Reconstruction (BIFR).

However, SICA and the BIFR—also called the "graveyard" of companies—failed to meet their objectives due to delays caused by litigation and a lack of timely decisions by stakeholders. The SICA was finally repealed in 2003, and some of its provisions were incorporated into the Companies Act, 2013, with the National Company Law Tribunal replacing the functions of the BIFR.

The Corporate Debt Restructuring (CDR) framework was launched on August 23, 2001, to provide a new mechanism for the timely and transparent restructuring of debt for viable entities, without the legacy issues of the BIFR, the Debt Recovery Tribunals (DRT), and other legal proceedings. The idea was to save viable companies and minimize losses to banks through a coordinated debt restructuring program.

> The CDR was one of the most successful tools
> that helped several sectors—such as steel and
> power—survive the downturn of the early 2000s.

The CDR was one of the most successful tools that helped several sectors—such as steel and power—survive the downturn of the early 2000s. It allowed many companies affected by external shocks to restructure their operations. Some of its biggest success stories include JSW Steel and Arvind Ltd., an Ahmedabad-based textile firm, demonstrating how corporate debt restructuring helped Indian companies survive economic downturns and external shocks.

DEBTORS-IN-POSSESSION VS. CREDITORS-IN-CONTROL

The Insolvency and Bankruptcy Code of 2016 was enacted to consolidate the existing frameworks for insolvency and bankruptcy. Since its creation, it has emerged as a significant tool for the recovery of bad loans, according to the Reserve Bank of India.

However, this new law follows the British system of "creditors-in-control" to resolve the debt of a defaulting company. This contrasts with the American debt resolution process, where the debtor remains "in possession" of the company, and has the powers and duties of a trustee.

In the American system, the company owner is allowed to operate the business and may, with court approval, borrow more. A plan of reorganization is proposed, and creditors whose rights are affected are allowed to vote on the plan. The plan is confirmed by the court if it receives the required votes and meets certain legal requirements.

Popularly known as a "Chapter 11" filing, the debt resolution process of the United States Bankruptcy Code begins with a petition filed with the bankruptcy court. This petition may be voluntary—filed by the borrower, or involuntary—filed by the creditors.

> Unlike the insolvency law in India, which does not give a second chance for the promoter to help reorganize the debt, the American system enlists the help of the promoter to restructure the company.

Unlike the insolvency law in India, which does not give a second chance for the promoter to help reorganize the debt, the American system enlists the help of the promoter to restructure the company. The idea behind the American law is that the founder or owner of a company is more knowledgeable about the company's customers, suppliers, and financial intricacies than a newly appointed resolution professional who has no prior connection to the company.

For example, when Apple—one of the world's biggest technology companies—was on the brink of bankruptcy in 1997, software major Microsoft came forward with a $150 million investment. Co-founder Steve Jobs was brought back as CEO, and since then, Apple has broken sales records with the launch of new and innovative products. This is one of the most successful turnarounds in the history of global companies.

Similar examples can be found in India, where several companies, especially in cyclical industries like steel and power, sought loan restructuring from their lenders to remain in business. The government and banks realized that any company can default on its loans due to various external reasons beyond its control. The cancellation of second-generation wireless telephony licences by the Supreme Court in February 2012, for instance, caused several companies to default on loans. This affected not only the telecom companies but also their suppliers.

External factors such as natural disasters, adverse court judgments, and changes in laws in other countries can cause a company to incur losses. For example, the business models of several coal-based power stations in India changed overnight after Indonesia—a major coal supplier—hiked duties on coal exports in October 2013. This resulted in losses for electricity generation companies like Tata Power's Mundra plant and Gujarat-based power stations of Essar and Adani. These companies could only remain viable after restructuring their loans, and passing on the increased electricity tariffs to various state boards, as suggested by the Supreme Court.

Bankers argue that if a company has robust internal audit systems and no evidence of fund diversion, the business owners should be given an opportunity to reorganize their debt, in a similar manner to the American bankruptcy resolution process.

UNDERSTANDING TURNAROUND MANAGEMENT

Even in the face of overpowering circumstances, several Indian companies have had stellar comebacks. This is frequently thanks to various loan restructuring schemes, court judgements, and the high quality of new management.

Let's take the case of cyclical industries like steel and power, where companies periodically undergo arduous challenges that could shut them down.

The Tatas took over the failing Bhushan Steel plant in Odisha in May 2018 for ₹35,200 crore; soon, they turned around Bhushan Steel's operations by taking a series of steps while retaining the old team.

A year later, the world's biggest steel maker—ArcelorMittal—and Nippon Steel of Japan acquired Essar

Steel's Hazira plant in Gujarat, the same gas-based one we mentioned earlier. This 10 million tonnes per annum plant was sold for ₹42,000 crore and became a huge success story of the new IBC law.

JSW Steel acquired Bhushan Power and Steel Limited in March 2021 for ₹19,350 crore. Within a couple of years, the Sajjan Jindal led group successfully turned around its operations. We'll be looking at the turnarounds of Bhushan Steel by Tata, and Bhushan Power by JSW in greater detail in the first two chapters of this book. These companies were able to bring about their turnarounds due to the high quality of their top management.

Professor Himanshu Rai, Director of the Indian Institute of Management, Indore, told Dev Chatterjee in an interview in January 2023 that Indian businesses today face constant disruption; companies can experience losses and failures on ventures that were promising, just a few years ago. "Instead of closing down the underperforming units, business leaders can carry out a turnaround exercise with a carefully crafted strategy. Turnaround management is an essential part of any organization's strategic endeavours," Rai asserts.

So what exactly does turnaround management involve?

According to Rai, the obvious first step is acknowledging the issues of the underperforming ventures, identifying the reasons behind these, and then, committing to diagnose them. "This requires strong data forecasting abilities, trend analyses, and frequent audits. Identifying key areas requiring action is crucial. For example, Dabur India redesigned its growth strategy under the leadership of its CEO Sunil Duggal, and successfully turned around its performance," Rai notes.

Strategists then need to design a blueprint that uses all tools within budget constraints. This calls for restructuring, forming new partnerships, innovation, diversification, and rebranding. An example is Bharti Airtel, which turned around by cutting costs, forming partnerships, and focusing on customer service.

Rai suggests that a CEO must balance experimentation with proven methods, but the focus should always be on creating value for customers. Tata Motors—which made huge losses due to its small car Nano—turned around by cutting costs, launching new products, and focusing on customer satisfaction.

Tata Motors—which made huge losses due to its small car Nano—turned around by cutting costs, launching new products, and focusing on customer satisfaction.

"Restructuring requires strong leadership committed to making bold decisions and ensuring effective strategy implementation. A leader should take a proactive approach and be able to make quick difficult decisions. Communication and building trust with stakeholders are also crucial," Rai says.

Anu Aga, the former chairman of Thermax, successfully turned around the company by reorganizing its business plan and breaking it into six primary businesses, after an anonymous letter criticized the firm for its inaction.

Turnaround strategies come in various forms and can include the sale of an asset, diversification into new areas, restructuring, layoffs, redesign, reengineering, and retraining of employees.

While quick action is often essential, a long-term sustainability plan is also necessary. Rai maintains that the initial plan must be expanded and upgraded after its evaluation.

A turnaround strategy requires strong leadership, vision, commitment, forecasting ability, and an understanding of the market, the industry, and customers. The business leaders described in the following chapters show these traits in abundance.

A turnaround strategy requires strong leadership, vision, commitment, forecasting ability, and an understanding of the market, the industry, and customers.

There are also examples of Indian companies which turned around while still under the same management. Arvind Ltd., an Ahmedabad-based textile company, made a spectacular turnaround led by the Sanjay Lalbhai family after its debt was restructured by Indian banks.

"The key factor is the leader's ability to create trust and capability within their team and organization. In the Indian context, it is imperative to have a deep understanding of the market and industry to achieve successful turnarounds," Rai states.

There are several other instances where Indian entrepreneurs managed to turn around their companies despite adverse external circumstances. While there are indeed a few bad apples in Corporate India, there are also companies which have reversed their fortunes to give adequate returns to all stakeholders.

In an interview with the author in early 2023, DVR Seshadri, a professor at the Indian School of Business (ISB)—an iconic management school in Hyderabad—cited the example of Tata Steel to highlight how the company decided to fight back once the steel industry was opened up for competition.

The Tata group, under its patriarch Ratan Tata, decided to invest more money into the company. "The leadership put extreme focus on a few strategic themes, to consolidate before expansion. To do so, it sought to start the turnaround journey by identifying its areas of strength and leveraging them," says Professor Seshadri.

"Tata Steel had captive raw material resources and embarked on process innovation. The company ushered in performance orientation. Leveraging this new performance culture, the headcount of the organization was right-sized in an extremely humane manner," Seshadri notes.

Realizing that culture change across such a large company would be a challenge, Tata Steel sought to bring the new culture into a new plant it was setting up, which became a role model for the rest of the company to emulate. Tata Steel's Managing Director TV Narendran's account of how he turned around the company is featured in this book.

India Inc's Greatest Turnarounds showcases the success stories of some Indian companies that managed to turn around their prospects by changing their strategies in finance, marketing, and human resources.

As India marches towards a $30 trillion economy by 2047, it requires new legions of entrepreneurs.

As India marches towards a $30 trillion economy by 2047, it requires new legions of entrepreneurs. Some of these entrepreneurs will also fail, but it's important that all stakeholders come forward to help their companies survive. After all, a dead company is not good news for any stakeholder.

1.

JSW STEEL

Back from the Brink

It was the summer of 2022, when the race to acquire Swiss materials firm Holcim's stake in India's Ambuja Cement was at its peak. Apart from the Adani and Aditya Birla Groups, the Sajjan Jindal owned JSW group had also joined the race.

Both the Birla and JSW groups already had a significant presence in the cement industry. But for the Adani group, acquisition of Ambuja Cement and its subsidiary ACC—an 87-year old company—would have made it India's second largest player with a capacity of 70 million tonnes per annum (MTPA). The competition, therefore, was intense with the bidders burning the midnight oil to strike a deal.

As bankers, lawyers, and auditors began hectic negotiations in Mumbai, Zurich, and London, the Indian billionaires—Sajjan Jindal, Kumar Mangalam Birla, and Gautam Adani—flew across continents to negotiate with the Holcim team, and with banks to raise funds.

An interview by Jindal with *The Financial Times* on May 10, 2022, increased the tempo among the bidders. JSW group,

Jindal said, would make a $7 billion offer for Ambuja Cement and ACC with $4.5 billion of its own equity and $2.5 billion from undisclosed private equities. The acquisition would be a "game changer" for JSW Cement which had a capacity of 17 MTPA, Jindal told the FT.

But within days, in a surprise decision, Holcim announced that the Adani Group would acquire its entire stakes in Ambuja Cement and ACC in an all-cash deal of $10.5 billion. Of this, Adani would pay $6.4 billion to Holcim, and the rest of the cash would be used to buy shares from minority shareholders of Ambuja Cement and ACC, under the mandatory open offer.

Jindal, who had offered more cash than Adani, had lost the race. The CEO of Holcim, Jan Jenisch, later clarified to analysts that JSW and Birla Ultratech's offers were rejected due to the potential delays in getting Competition Commission of India's approvals, as both have sprawling cement companies.

It was a big chance lost for Jindal to make a dent in the Indian cement industry, and to take on market leader Ultratech. But the setback did not deter Jindal, who built a $22 billion revenue empire from other acquisition opportunities. This was not the first time the 64-year-old had faced adverse circumstances—Jindal was down but not out.

Walking into JSW Group's swanky glass and steel headquarters in Mumbai's Bandra Kurla Complex, one can see the group's transformation from a small steel company of the 1980s to a conglomerate with a presence in power generation, infrastructure, cement, paints, sports, and venture capital, besides steel.

The aesthetically designed headquarters has become a symbol of success for Jindal, who took on several pathbreaking steps and huge risks when the Indian economy was just opening up to compete on a global level in 1991, after the stifling "licence raj". When Sajjan Jindal set up his first steel plant at Vijayanagar in North Karnataka, no one could have predicted that JSW Steel would become the second biggest steel producer in India (after Tata Steel at 35 MTPA), with a production capacity of 28.5 MTPA, as per the company's annual report

> When Sajjan Jindal set up his first steel plant at Vijayanagar in North Karnataka, no one could have predicted what JSW Steel would become— the second biggest steel producer in India.

Born on December 5, 1959, in Kolkata, Sajjan Jindal studied Mechanical Engineering at Bangalore University. Right out of college in 1982, Jindal joined his father's company— OP Jindal Group—in Bengaluru. He was soon moved into the western region operations division in Mumbai, to look after the group's steel manufacturing business. In 1989, Jindal started Jindal Iron and Steel Company (JISCO) to manufacture cold rolled and galvanized sheet products.

Jindal was betting on producing steel in Karnataka, which had good stores of iron ore—the raw material required to make steel. Sajjan Jindal was keen to start a factory in Vijayanagar, in rural North Karnataka, a barren and underdeveloped region. Despite its complete lack of infrastructure and skilled manpower, this is where Jindal envisioned his pet project. He called it the Jindal Vijayanagar Steel Limited (JVSL).

Jindal set up a new team of engineers and finance professionals to start working on his Vijayanagar steel project. Incorporated in this project was the latest Corex technology imported from Austria, the first of its kind to make its way into India.

The Indian steel sector was until then dominated by the century old Tata Steel and the government-owned Steel Authority of India (SAIL). Existing steel producers were comfortable with their current manufacturing processes, using available yet obsolete technology. Jindal's strategy of importing new and more efficient technology was a pioneering effort in the game. At the time, only two other companies used Corex technology worldwide.

To make steel, iron ore is first processed by smelters in the blast furnace. Liquid hot iron metal is produced, and is

Jindal's strategy of importing new and more efficient technology was a pioneering effort in the game.

converted to steel. In the steel mills, the liquid steel is first cast into slabs, and then rolled into coils. JVSL, however, began the production process backwards by first starting the steel mill and acquiring the slabs. JVSL was buying slabs from the market to run the steel plant, to produce and sell hot rolled coils.

JVSL started the backwards integration by first commissioning the Corex technology, followed by the construction of the blast furnace, and finally the pellet plant. To initiate the steel-manufacturing process, Corex unit one was commissioned in August 1998.

A big advantage of using Corex technology in the steel company was that it did not require expensive coking coal. Instead, an inferior quality of coal could be used to run the plant. Thus, the steel plant would be run by using only 15 per cent of coking coal, with the rest being lower-priced coal, resulting in huge cost savings for the company.

Besides, the Corex technology-based steel mill would also release more hot gases, which could be used to produce electricity. Hence, not only was the cost of production lower with this technology, it also replaced higher-cost imported energy requirements for the mill, resulting in savings in foreign exchange.

Among Jindal's A-team was Seshagiri Rao, the Group MD and go-to man for finance, who was tasked with negotiating with lenders to raise funds for Vijayanagar. The new steel mill project was to be funded by promoter's contribution, sale of shares to retail shareholders, and bank debt.

> When JVSL knocked on the doors of Indian lenders to raise funds for the project, it was met with scepticism about the Corex technology proposed for its steel plant.

When JVSL knocked on the doors of Indian lenders to raise funds for the project, it was met with scepticism about the Corex technology proposed for its steel plant. After all, there had been no need for Corex in the huge Tata and SAIL steel plants the lenders were familiar with. "There was no template, no past records or any literature to support that this new technology would work in India," recalls Rao, a soft-spoken affable man, in an interview with the author at JSW's sprawling headquarters in Mumbai.

After conducting several feasibility studies on how the new Corex technology would help the steel industry, the lenders—led by IDBI—finally agreed to fund JVSL's steel plant. An excited Jindal and his team rushed to Vijayanagar by catching an overnight train from Mumbai to commission the project.

But as soon as the brand new steel plant crackled to life in August 1998, disaster struck.

LIKE FATHER, LIKE SON

Sajjan Jindal inherited his fearless pioneering spirit from his father. Om Prakash Jindal—the patriarch of the Jindal family—was born in August 1930 to a farmer's family. He grew up in a small village called Nalwa in Haryana. The country was still 17 years away from gaining independence from the British empire, and a vast majority of Indians, including OP's father, were agriculturists. A few textile mills owned by the Birlas, and steel plants and power companies owned by the Tatas lorded over the Indian industrial empire.

OP Jindal moved to a nearby town for further education. Once India gained independence, OP (as he was popularly known) relocated to Calcutta (now Kolkata). In 1964, he set up a manufacturing business under the name Jindal (India) Limited, making pipe bends and sockets. Later, OP set up his first big factory in Calcutta, called Jindal Strips. This was the beginning of an empire which has now spread across the world, with OP Jindal's four sons running their own independent ventures.

OP's eldest son, Prithvi Raj Jindal, is the Chairman of the pipes company Jindal SAW, while Sajjan Jindal spearheads the JSW Group. Ratan Jindal is running the operations of Jindal Stainless, while the youngest among the brothers, Naveen Jindal—a former member of parliament from Congress—leads Jindal Steel and Power.

The OP Jindal Group was among the first business organizations to see a vast potential in regions such as Hisar, Haryana; Raigarh in Chhattisgarh; Kutch, Gujarat; Vizag in Andhra Pradesh; Bellary in Karnataka; as well as Vasind and Tarapur in Maharashtra. The group continuously integrated its operations backwards, moving from pipe bends to manufacturing pipes, then to steel and to power. Subsequently, the group went into infrastructure to tap into the growing opportunities thrown up in independent India.

In 1991, with the support of Congress, OP Jindal joined politics and was elected to the Haryana Assembly. When he became a Member of Parliament after winning the Lok Sabha election from Kurukshetra in 1996, OP asked his four sons to take over the reins of separate group companies.

However, in a shocking accident, OP Jindal died in a helicopter crash in March 2005, within days of being appointed as Power Minister of the Haryana state government. He was 75. The Jindal brothers were devastated.

THE "ARCHITECT OF CDR"

When Sajjan Jindal brought Corex technology to manufacture steel in India, he was quite bullish about its future. But within days of installation of the plant at Vijayanagar, water seeped inside the furnace and froze the metal in it. The plant had to be shut down.

Rao, the top lieutenant of Jindal, recalls those early days when the Corex technology at their Bellary plant appeared faulty. "As soon as the Corex technology failed, our lenders stopped the disbursement of loans. As a result, we failed to pay our contractors—like L&T—who were working at the site. We started to analyze what went wrong with Corex even when it was a success story in the rest of the world," Rao says.

The lenders were very apprehensive about this project that utilized a new technology. They were unwilling to offer more funds, especially as the steel plant had shut down. By now, half the project was commissioned and the rest was under construction. From a prospective highly profitable business venture, JVSL now seemed likely to become a stalled project.

The company's investigations revealed that the Corex did not fail due to any errors in the technology itself; instead, the issue was caused by Indian weather. As Bellary was an arid region, the project consultant had built the conveyor belts (that carried iron ore and coal to the plant) without any covering to keep the goods dry. There was no protection from rain for the raw materials as they made their way to the plant.

But just as JVSL started up the project in August 1998, Vijayanagar saw extreme weather, with heavy rains drenching northern Karnataka. Rao notes, "It was not the technology, but we found out that the design itself was flawed. Due to scanty rainfall in the area, no one had expected heavy rains." The company asked the lenders to continue bankrolling the project since its errors could be fixed, but they did not agree. "We had a serious crisis on our hands even before the project earned a single rupee," Rao recalls.

Armed with several documents and reports from similar plants across the world, JVSL officials led by Jindal met lenders to convince them about the technology. After several meetings, the lenders decided to appoint an independent agency to study the problem, and suggest solutions.

This was also the time when Jindal had already invested his cash in equity as part of his 63 per cent stake. The company had earlier come out with a public issue in 1994 to raise around ₹1,100 crore in cash from the public. As per the guidelines of the market regulator—the Securities and Exchange Board of India (SEBI)—a company implementing a greenfield project could not raise the entire money at one go; instead it had to raise funds bit by bit, corresponding to the progress of the project.

As per the guidelines of the market regulator—the Securities and Exchange Board of India (SEBI)—a company implementing a greenfield project could not raise the entire money at one go.

Based on the project's requirements, the company had raised ₹2.50 per share on application for ₹10 a share, and ₹2.50 was to be collected on allotment. The rest of the money was to be raised on calls. Between 1994 and 1997, the company did not raise the remaining half of the money, as it did not require any money then. But due to the furnace-related crisis, the share price fell to an all-time low of ₹2 a share. And despite several calls and reminders, the retail shareholders did not send in their cheques.

As there was no infusion of additional equity, lenders stopped financing the project, and to make matters worse, the plant had stopped production. The company still managed to buy slabs, rolling them into coils and selling these to maintain its cash flows. The company went for backward integration at its Vasind and Tarapur plants, which were thankfully making money.

The lenders eventually appointed a consultant and Roland Berger's team came to India to study the project. After almost nine months, the consultant recommended several steps for the company to restart the project.

In the meantime, the company made an insurance claim for the Corex fiasco but the claim was rejected on technical grounds. The company still managed to pay salaries and to meet other expenditures from its meagre cash flows.

The lenders informed Jindal that if he were to put in more equity, they would be able to fund the stalled project.

However, many construction contractors who had left the site due to delayed payments were unwilling to go back to the project. The lenders, who were keen to see the project take off, said they would pay the contractors their past dues if they completed their work at the site. Armed with a letter from the banks and a promise that they would pay all past dues with interest, the company convinced the contractors to restart construction at the project site.

> By August of 1999, the Corex technology-led project was back on track, and within 15 days, the plant had reached its peak production capacity.

By August of 1999, the Corex technology-led project was back on track, and within 15 days, the plant had reached its peak production capacity. Despite all the hiccups caused by several financial and operational glitches, and even truant weather, Jindal had finally managed to hit the target.

The next challenge for Jindal was to start the second phase of his Corex steel project. The company officials met the lenders and sought their help to start the second phase, which was crucial to the financial viability of the entire project. The lenders agreed and the company finally completed the project by 2001.

Although the plant was now commissioned, Jindal soon realized that all its financial ratios had gone haywire—the company would not be able to repay its bank debt. The average interest rates for the project were hovering at a steep 16.7 per cent, thus hitting the bottom-line of the young company.

The company informed the lenders that despite the project now producing steel at full capacity, it would not be able to service the debt. Restructuring of debt by lenders would be essential to salvage the company.

The lenders agreed to debt restructuring by sacrificing a part of their interest income, but not without a condition—Jindal would have to make a bigger investment in the company in the form of equity. "We had no money to put into the company... that's when Corporate Debt Restructuring (CDR) was launched in 2002 to save Indian companies which had a promising future but were facing problems due to unavoidable reasons. We were, in a way, the architects of CDR in India," Rao says, about the company's ₹6,000 crore debt restructuring.

In order to get the lenders to agree to the CDR, Jindal offered to write down promoter equity from 63 per cent to 40 per cent. The lenders, on the other hand, agreed to convert part of their debt into 40 per cent stake in the company.

The lenders also agreed to bring down their average rate of interest to 10.8 per cent from 17 per cent. A part of the Indian currency denominated loan was converted into foreign currency at a lower interest rate of 8 per cent.

The CDR was implemented in such a way that a part of the loan attracted zero per cent coupon, while lenders asked the company to pay 14 per cent interest on remaining loans.

The lenders also had the right to recompense, i.e., if the company did well in future, the lenders would have to be compensated. As a final condition, the lenders sought Jindal's personal guarantee. The CDR was cleared in 2002 by the lenders—and JSW became the template for the rest of India Inc. to follow.

The CDR was cleared in 2002 by the lenders—and JSW became the template for the rest of India Inc. to follow.

The stock markets reacted positively to the management's sincerity. This was followed by more good news from an unexpected quarter. China, which had joined the World Trade Organization (WTO) in December 2001, started a rally in the commodities cycle with its huge demand for steel.

With its steel plant operating at full capacity, the company was able to meet its financial commitments to the lenders comfortably. Its financial ratios improved with its EBITDA (Earnings before interest, tax, depreciation and amortization) hovering at a healthy six to one. EBITDA is a metric used to evaluate a company's operating performance and is an indicator of cash flow from the company's operations.

This was at a time when lenders put several restrictions on the company's expansion, including a ban on incurring capital expenditure beyond ₹40 crore. Any additional capital expenditure had to be cleared by the lenders first, as they were worried that further outlays might result in higher debt for the company.

In these circumstances, while the company was producing at full capacity, it still did not have the blast furnace in place. A blast furnace is an important component of steel-making which is in the form of a tower—within it, rocks containing iron ore are melted to produce steel.

To construct a new blast furnace, the company would have to invest an additional ₹400 crore. This would have helped the company to take its production capacity to 2.5 MTPA from 1.6 MTPA. The company could therefore increase the plant's capacity at a relatively small cost.

In an innovative move, the company approached local steel traders with a proposal to raise funds. The traders were informed that JVSL had two projects under construction—a coke oven and a blast furnace.

The cash-rich steel traders were asked to invest 50 per cent equity in both the projects, with a total investment of ₹200 crore. The project would be completed in 12-18 months, with a guaranteed 20 per cent return on equity. At the same time, the company assured the lenders that the existing cash flows of JVSL would remain untouched for the two new projects.

The company argued that commissioning of the coke oven and blast furnace would, on the contrary, increase the cash flows even after paying 20 per cent returns to the steel traders. Even if the two projects were to fail, Jindal promised that JVSL was ring-fenced from any negative consequences.

"We told the lenders that if we got extra cash flow to the company due to the two projects, then the lenders would have the full right to use the extra cash to reduce the company's debt. As the risk for the new project was taken by the steel traders and not by JVSL, the lenders could not find any reasons to say no," Rao recalls. The project was completed by 2004; the company's cash flow increased substantially, as promised by the management.

> The stock markets reacted positively to the company's efforts at reducing its debt, and its share prices jumped to ₹100 from its low of ₹2 a share.

The stock markets reacted positively to the company's efforts at reducing its debt, and its share prices jumped to ₹100 from its low of ₹2 a share. Lenders who were holding JVSL's equity made a huge profit on their shares; their losses due to the CDR scheme were well compensated by the high share price.

Jindal had the right to buy back shares from the lenders in a way such that the banks would not book any losses even for the pre-CDR interest rates. The company gave two options to the lenders: they could either exercise the right to recompense, or retain their shares.

As the share price was high, most of the lenders decided to retain their stake. The company managed to exit the CDR with the lenders making a hefty profit on their 40 per cent stake. Since then, as they say, Jindal has never looked back.

Enthused by the success of their first ever CDR, the lenders got back in touch with Jindal in a few months, in 2005. They asked him whether he would be interested in taking over SISCOL, a loss-making steel plant in Salem, Tamil Nadu. The unit was owned by the Lakshmi Machine Works (LMW) group. LMW had set up the Salem unit to manufacture long products. In steel industry terminology, 'long products' refers to steel products such as wires, rods, rails, and bars, as well as different types of steel structural sections and girders.

"The lenders asked us to take over the loss-making unit at an equity of just ₹1, which turned out to be a big game changer for us," Rao says. The Salem unit had a debt of ₹1,000 crore, and the lenders were not interested in taking a haircut on their dues. So, in talks with the JSW Group, the lenders negotiated a new instrument called Optionally Convertible Debentures (OCDs) to be issued by JSW at ₹62 a share.

The instrument was available to the lenders in the first five years, or with the issuer in case JSW wanted to merge the Salem unit with their existing unit. If JSW did not merge the unit, then they would pay 2 per cent interest on the OCDs to the tune of ₹600 crore. If there were no merger, after five years the instrument would pay 10 per cent interest, with retrospective effect.

"It was a good deal for the lenders, and we were having the gut feeling that we would do very well in the company (SISCOL) and the share price would remain above ₹62 a share," Rao reminisces about JSW's first acquisition. "We took over the company and we completely converted it to a specialty steel company. The share price went up to ₹100, and then we announced the merger of the unit with the parent company."

The group also decided to merge its Vasind and Tarapur units with the parent company in the same year, and at the same time, increase the capacity of SISCOL to 1 MTPA. With this, JSW's total capacity touched 3.5 MTPA. The group now decided to raise production capacity at the Vijayanagar site in phases.

By 2010, the company started negotiating with Ispat Steel, a loss-making unit owned by Pramod Mittal—a well-known industrialist and the younger brother of ArcelorMittal's chairman, LN Mittal. Ispat Steel had defaulted on its loans; its lenders were not convinced by the management's attempts to revive the company.

The lenders asked Jindal and Tata Steel to conduct due diligence if they were interested in Ispat Steel. Jindal made a no-haircuts offer to the lenders that inclined them towards JSW. The acquisition of Ispat Steel for ₹2,157 crore made JSW Steel the largest steelmaker in India, with its capacity rising to 14.3 MTPA by the financial year ending March 2011.

The Ispat unit was turned around within three years of acquisition, and it was merged with JSW Steel by 2013.

"We learnt our biggest lesson from our own experience between 1997 and 2000—that financial prudence is very important. Whether it was our expansion or acquisitions, we never faltered on our financial ratios. We always remained within the 3.75 debt to EBITDA ratio and 1.75 times debt to net worth ratio," Rao declares. "This was sacrosanct and we never moved away from these ratios."

According to Rao, since 2005, several good governance practices were introduced with the induction of independent directors like former Finance Secretary, Vijay Kelkar, into the board. That was the reason JSW remained unscathed when the Lehman crisis hit, even as many of its rivals faced hardships due to the tightening of global markets. Some of the acquisitions made in the United States and Chile in 2008-09 by JSW Group, however, did not go well.

"But compared to the acquisitions in India, the overseas acquisitions were not so big as to bring us down. In India, whatever we touched became gold for us, but not overseas," Rao concedes.

After 2013, the company started expanding organically. With its capacity at Vijayanagar going up from 2.5 MTPA to 6.8 MTPA at the time of the global financial crisis, it was further raised to 10 MTPA by 2013. The company also started aggressively expanding at SISCOL in Tamil Nadu and in the Ispat Steel unit in Dolvi, Maharashtra. JSW reached a total capacity of 23 MTPA—almost on par with market leader Tata Steel, which too had been recently increasing its production.

PROJECT SALBONI–A NON-STARTER

In 2008, JSW Steel had decided to set up a 10 MTPA steel project in Salboni, 152 km east of Kolkata, at the cost of ₹35,000 crore. The project, however, started on an inauspicious note. When Chief Minister Buddhadeb Bhattacharjee was driving back moments after laying the foundation stone for the steel plant, suspected Naxals bombed the road—16 km from the JSW project site. While the politician and his colleagues were unharmed, several accompanying policemen were injured.

> When Chief Minister Buddhadeb Bhattacharjee was driving back moments after laying the foundation stone for the steel plant, suspected Naxals bombed the road—16 km from the JSW project site.

Jindal had proposed to offer shares in the company to land owners in the region—thus making them partners in the project. "I am a farmer's son. I can understand," Jindal had famously said even as Tata Motors' Nano project had to shift from Bengal to Gujarat due to violent protests by local farmers.

But the Naxals—an underground political movement in East and Central India dating back to the 1960s—were protesting the land acquisition from farmers and the lack of opportunities for landless farmers. On September 30, 2009, the rebels killed three members of the ruling Communist Party of India, after kidnapping them from Salboni.

In 2011, Mamata Banerjee, a firebrand local leader, took over as chief minister of West Bengal. She publicly expressed her disapproval for the delays in the Salboni project. It was then found that the company had not signed lease agreements with the previous state government. Around 4,300 acres had been allocated by Buddhadeb's government. Of this, JSW had purchased 450 acres directly from the farmers in a peaceful manner.

Apart from slow acquisition of land, lack of iron ore for the project became a big hurdle for the project. Mamata Banerjee then issued an ultimatum to JSW for starting this project.

In August 2014, in response to Banerjee's threat, JSW Group told *Business Standard*—a business daily—that they were committed to the project and had already spent over ₹600 crore on it. "Unfortunately, iron ore, which is the critical input for steel-making, is not made available to steel companies which are set up after liberalization, for value addition within India. Instead, India granted mining concessions to merchant miners encouraging export of iron ore and import of steel," the group had explained.

Compounding the problem, the group said, iron ore-bearing states like Jharkhand and Odisha were not supplying the ore, thus stalling the operation of steel companies. "In these circumstances, JSW Steel requested the West Bengal government to facilitate long-term supply of iron ore to take up active implementation of its project," the *Business Standard* quoted JSW Steel officials.

A senior minister commented to the *Business Standard* that JSW was not interested in the Salboni project; they kept asking about iron ore which was not the state government's problem. As the project seemed to be a long way off, JSW had proposed to the West Bengal government that it be allowed to use coal from allocated mines for its project in Karnataka instead. "We made it very clear that the coal mines were allocated through the state dispensation route and could not be routed to Bellary. Our hunch was that the company was only interested in the coal mines," the government official told the paper.

As per the agreement, the coking coal mine was meant for the steel plant, while the non-coking coal was to be used for the captive power plant. Any surplus power had to be sold to the West Bengal State Electricity Board under a power purchase agreement.

The paper noted that the captive power plant was to be set up jointly by JSW Steel and JSW Energy. The project was to be developed by a new company in which JSW Steel was to pick up 26 per cent stake while its sister company, JSW Energy, was to own the rest. By the third quarter of 2011, JSW Energy sold its stake in the coal mines in favour of JSW Bengal Steel. However, this did not help the project pick up pace.

In 2014, the Supreme Court cancelled the allocation of two coal mines by the state government to JSW's steel and power plant, in a case that deemed such allotment by states to corporations as illegal. This finally sealed the fate of the steel and power project. JSW was sitting on a huge plot of land, with no business plans.

In 2014, the Supreme Court cancelled the allocation of two coal mines by the state government to JSW's steel and power plant, in a case that deemed such allotment by states to corporations as illegal.

The company went back to the drawing board to restructure the entire project. It did not have favourable conditions to expand in the east. The ₹35,000 crore project was not only stalled, but a new solution needed to be found to accommodate the aspirations of the local people, and for the company which had already sunk a lot of money.

By January 2016, the company came up with the idea to set up a cement plant at the site to produce 2.4 MTPA of cement at an investment of ₹800 crore. A 300 MW power plant was also announced by Banerjee who laid the foundation stone of the cement plant.

"The Salboni unit supports our nation-building goals. Today's inaugural function marks a significant milestone for both the JSW Group and West Bengal. West Bengal has been a preferred state for setting up one of our biggest cement manufacturing units. We are committed to stay invested in this state and are, in fact, planning to increase the capacity of our Salboni cement unit to 3.6 MTPA. This will create new employment opportunities and community initiatives at Salboni", said Parth Jindal, son of Sajjan Jindal, who was leading the cement project.

"The Salboni unit's capacity expansion is part of our goal to achieve an overall production capacity of 20 MTPA by 2020. We take immense pride in dedicating the Salboni cement unit to the economic development of West Bengal," Jindal said. By 2019, JSW was planning to expand cement capacity to 25 MTPA but by the summer of 2023, its capacity remained at 17 MTPA as it missed the acquisition of Ambuja Cement and ACC by a whisker.

NEW TURNAROUND OPPORTUNITIES
VIA THE IBC

In 2016, the Indian government introduced the Insolvency
and Bankruptcy Code to clean up the balance sheets of
banks which were inundated with a mountain of bad debts.
Many steel and electricity generation companies were
unable to repay their debt due to adverse court judgements,
as well changes in policies in India and overseas.

Some companies which were sent for debt resolution
under the new bankruptcy law were accused by the
government's investigative agencies of fraud and fund
diversion, committed by promoters of these bankrupt
companies.

Steel companies with strong balance sheets, such as JSW
Steel, Tata Steel, and the world's largest steel company,
ArcelorMittal, saw this as a big opportunity to expand their
businesses in India. JSW Group, which had lost a chance
to venture east with its ₹35,000 crore steel project in West
Bengal, saw a new opening to extend into eastern India.

Lenders sent certain large steel companies like Essar
Steel, Bhushan Steel and Bhushan Power & Steel (Bhushan
Power for short) to the bankruptcy court as they had failed
to repay their debts. Some of the smaller companies for
sale included Electrosteel, Usha Ispat, and Monnet Ispat.

Jindal was eyeing Bhushan Steel, Bhushan Power, and Monnet Ispat for acquisition. So were others.

JSW had a good conversion cost of $115 per tonne of steel making, making it one of the most cost efficient commodities in the world. The company also had a good track record of project implementation and could deploy lower capital to expand capacity. The company became very efficient in terms of interest and depreciation—the key financial ratios for expanding their business.

"These were the two distinct advantages for us. The company was able to pass through the cycles even when many of our rival companies were restructured," Rao contends. "Despite buying coal and iron ore from the market, the company was profitable when compared to others. Dumping of steel by China impacted prices all over the world and sent financial metrics of several companies into a tailspin," Rao recalls about the 2016 down cycle for the industry. Prior to this, the Supreme Court had issued a ruling that banned iron ore mining in Bellari, Karnataka, since 2011, which made matters worse.

While most steel companies went downhill, JSW was able to tide over the crisis as it managed its financials better, besides keeping its capital and conversion costs low. "These were the three main strengths which kept us in the business while the others failed to repay their debt," Rao said. Lenders were looking at huge losses from the steel industry.

JSW then decided to tie up with JFE Steel of Japan to produce automotive steel for the Indian market.

JSW then decided to tie up with JFE Steel of Japan to produce automotive steel for the Indian market. The Indian automobile market was booming and JSW wished to profit off this drive in demand, but lacked the technology. JFE Steel decided to offer its technology for an equity stake in the company. Additionally, JFE invested $1 billion into the company and obtained 15 per cent equity. This money was also used to buy Ispat Steel.

As a result, JSW's share in automotive steel went up from being nil to 33 per cent today. "The tie-up with JFE was a very good change in terms of benchmarking efficiencies and the technology, which helped us to move to the highest value chain," Rao says.

The company was able to produce different varieties of steel; value-added steel now contributes to almost 60 per cent of its total production. This has helped the company become less volatile in terms of margins, as compared to its competitors.

The company was initially focused on acquiring only three assets under the IBC. But if it succeeded in acquiring these three assets, then it would have been a significant burden on the company's balance sheet. The company therefore needed to create some joint ventures to make these acquisitions. "That's where the private equity firm Apollo came in," Rao recalls. Since it was founded in 1990 in New York, Apollo Global Management has become one of the largest asset managers in the world. As of December 2022, the company had $548 billion of assets under management and $99 billion invested in its private equity arm.

Apollo and JSW submitted a resolution plan for the bankrupt Monnet Ispat—they were successful in winning the company in September 2018.

Apollo and JSW submitted a resolution plan for the bankrupt Monnet Ispat—they were successful in winning the company in September 2018. The plant had already shut down and JSW had put in place a turnaround plan for the company. As a first step, the company restarted the pellet plant and the direct reduced iron (DRI) unit. The JSW management had realized that Monnet Ispat could be turned around by just starting these two units. The product offering was also changed to make specialty steel—on the lines of its Salem unit—by investing an additional ₹500 crore.

The company's units were gradually restarted over three years. Monnet Ispat reached its full capacity of two million tonnes and started to make money by the financial year ending in March 2022. The company was finally merged with the parent.

JSW was also interested in Bhushan Steel, but the Tatas made a better offer and managed to acquire the company by paying ₹35,200 crore to the lenders. Tata was also aggressive about acquiring Bhushan Power, but JSW made the winning bid of ₹19,700 crore versus Tata Steel's ₹16,000 crore. The acquisitions were not easy as litigation followed, for both Bhushan Steel and Bhushan Power, with former promoters raising several issues around the acquisitions by the Tatas as well as JSW.

Meanwhile, Britain's Liberty Steel had also entered the race to acquire Bhushan Power—the court ordered that its offer should be considered in the national interest, so as to get maximum value for the asset. Liberty Steel also took part in the race to acquire Essar Steel, in association with the Ruias—the promoters of the company who had defaulted on their loans. But ArcelorMittal emerged as the highest bidder, and its offer for Essar Steel was accepted by lenders.

By this time, all steel companies identified by the Reserve Bank of India in its first list of the "dirty dozen" loan defaulters were sold off; JSW had no option but to bid aggressively for Bhushan Power.

The company faced a legal tussle with the Liberty group of UK. As litigation over Bhushan Power progressed, Liberty

> All steel companies identified by the Reserve
> Bank of India in its first list of the "dirty dozen"
> loan defaulters were sold off; JSW had no option
> but to bid aggressively for Bhushan Power.

was late in providing bank guarantees to the lenders. The National Company Law Appellate Tribunal allowed all parties to submit fresh bids. JSW made an offer of ₹19,700 crore to the banks, and emerged as the highest bidder as against Bhushan Power's default of ₹48,000 crore to the lenders.

As soon as JSW took over Bhushan Power and Steel, they changed its procurement practices for coal and iron ore, integrating the procurement with the parent company.

Bhushan Power's sales were targeted at retail and not at the higher cash generating original equipment manufacturers. Besides, their sales to retail were at a huge discount. The new JSW management changed the sales strategy of Bhushan Power, and at the same time, also reduced costs substantially. JSW then decided to complete the stalled projects of Bhushan Power at a cost of ₹1,500 crore.

These projects, once implemented, helped to bring down costs substantially. The company used the additional cash to reduce its debt from ₹10,000 crore to ₹4,000 crore. The steel production capacity of Bhushan Power was also increased from 2.7 MTPA to 3.5 MTPA. The latest plan was to expand capacity to 5 MTPA by 2024.

The total steel capacity of JSW, including those from the acquisitions of Monnet Ispat and Bhushan Power, increased to 28 MTPA by the end of March 2023.

The total steel capacity of JSW, including those from the acquisitions of Monnet Ispat and Bhushan Power, increased to 28 MTPA by the end of March 2023. The company also has a steel capacity of 1.5 MTPA overseas.

As the demand for steel is rising exponentially, JSW Steel planned to increase capacity by another nine million tonnes, including at the Vijayanagar steel plant, by 2024.

Gopal Agrawal, former head of Investment Banking at Edelweiss, says JSW is one of the few groups that have successfully ventured into different sectors and expanded their presence beyond steel. "I have worked with them for a few transactions and truly believe that their success in M&A can be attributed to the vision and clarity of Jindal, and a very well-diversified and experienced senior team across functions and verticals. In addition to these, the most important (attribute) being their ability to raise funding for any M&A, be it equity or debt, given the reputation they enjoy with the private equity players and the whole lending community. This has ensured that funding is never an issue in their M&A journey," Agrawal observes.

While they have expanded their presence in multiple sectors, their intention has never been to remain a marginal player, but to build and strengthen their position in each of the segments over a period. While progressively expanding the group, Jindal has also kept the overall debt exposure in control, and ensured the right debt-equity balance.

> While progressively expanding the group, Jindal has also kept the overall debt exposure in control, and ensured the right debt-equity balance.

Taking a leaf from JSW Steel's books, Sajjan's other venture—JSW Energy—is also increasing its capacity via acquisitions. JSW Energy started its commercial operations in 2000 with the commissioning of its first 260 MW coal-based power plants near the steel plant site at Vijayanagar. Since then, the group made several acquisitions in the energy sector, to become an important player in the power industry. It's now the second largest company in the JSW Group.

In September 2015, JSW Energy acquired Himachal Baspa Power Company—the hydropower subsidiary of debt-laden Jaiprakash Power Ventures—for ₹9,275 crore. The Jaypee Group was crumbling under heavy debt and was shedding assets to repay banks.

The Jaypee acquisition, then one of the largest in the power sector, propelled JSW Energy into one of India's biggest private sector companies.

The Jaypee acquisition, then one of the largest in the power sector, propelled JSW Energy into one of India's biggest private sector companies. This also helped the group to move away from coal-based electricity generation towards the renewable energy space, giving it an advantage as an early mover.

Jindal says that with energy transition gaining momentum in recent years, the group has changed tracks; it aims to increase energy production to 20 GW by 2030, with almost 81 per cent via renewable energy sources.

"For the last two decades, JSW Energy has primarily been an electricity generation utility. However, as India gears for this transformative decade of serious action, it's time for us at JSW Energy to also enact change, and be at the forefront of energy transition," Jindal wrote to the company's shareholders in 2022.

"Therefore, over the next decade, I see our company transform from a power generating utility into an energy solutions provider for new green businesses such as energy storage and deep decarbonization. With a climate change agenda and sustainability at the core of our business, we remain committed to becoming a net-zero company by 2050," Jindal said about the future direction of the company.

In March 2023, JSW Neo Energy—a wholly-owned subsidiary of JSW Energy—said it acquired 1,753 MW of renewable energy assets from Mytrah Energy (India), and another 15 SPVs and 13 ancillary SPVs having 1,449 MW of total installed renewable energy capacity.

The transaction estimated Mytrah Energy's portfolio at an enterprise valuation of around ₹10,150 crores, and was the largest acquisition made by JSW Energy since its inception. The acquisition also helped the company to raise its current operational capacity by over 36 per cent from 4,811 MW to 6,564 MW.

The acquisition of Jaypee Group's hydropower projects and Mytrah Energy helped JSW create a strong foundation for its electricity generation and energy transition plans. The group's significant free cash flows are likely to facilitate it in achieving these targets without any equity dilution by the promoters—who own 74.66 per cent stake in the company.

Moreover, with about 2.9 GW of under-construction projects which are likely to be commissioned in phases over the next 12-18 months, JSW Energy is well ahead of its target to reach 10 GW capacity by the financial year ending March 2025, with the share of renewables increasing to 61 per cent.

SECRETS OF JSW'S TURNAROUND

Rao says an important step while turning around companies was to not change the existing management, including the CEOs. "We all sat together and compared the systems and work practices of JSW and the companies acquired by us. Whatever was good for either of the companies was implemented by the other. We never asked anybody to quit, but some top management officials like the chief of finance and marketing were sent from JSW Steel to Bhushan," Rao notes.

According to Rao, the secret sauce of any turnaround is to always remain on a path of growth, and to maintain financial prudence and transparency. "For instance, if I tell a lender this is what is happening in the company then that has to be true. Trust is very important. We could come out of many problems because we were always transparent with our lenders and stakeholders," says Rao.

"Besides, we never went back on our commitments. Once we tell our suppliers that we will repay their money in time, we never dishonoured our commitments. There has to be mutual trust with all the stakeholders—whether it is a customer or a vendor.

"At the same time, the basic business model should be profitable. If a business model is not profitable, whatever we do, it is of no use. That's the strength which Jindal has built in his company by creating some unique and distinctive advantages which are difficult for others to replicate. We focused on reducing conversion costs which is very difficult for some rivals to replicate," he asserts.

Rao makes some interesting revelations about the way JSW implements projects. "I'm not sure where else somebody can take the risk that Jindal can. For example, while starting a project, instead of outsourcing the entire project to a third party, we take charge of each department ourselves, and of its quality, which results in huge cost savings for us. We are conceptually different from others on project implementation. Once a project is complete, the project team moves to the next site to oversee the quality," Rao explains.

And so, the experienced staff of JSW has refined the procedure for improving the functioning of the new company. Rao adds, "When we take over a company, we implement a turnaround plan as per the standard operating procedure. For instance, Bhushan Power was running the older version of SAP operating system which was completely different from JSW's systems, as it was implementing SAP's latest version."

The procurement practices of the target company are also changed. For example, the site has no authority to make procurements in excess of ₹2 crore. This is done by the corporate office's central procurement team, which has a system of negotiation as a bulk procurer. Similarly, all decisions on capital expenditure above ₹2 crore are made at the headquarters.

At the same time the corporate office has to be nimble, not taking too much time to take decisions. While bigger decisions are made by the corporate office, day to day decisions are to be taken at the site, to keep things efficient.

In an interview with *Fortune India* in 2011, Jindal had said that challenging the status quo was the philosophy of his life. He would never give up easily. "When you go through a downturn, instead of becoming demoralized and depressed, it's better to think in a positive way," he declared.

The JSW Group will therefore continue to look at more acquisitions in the years to come, including making a foray into the electric vehicle segment.

The JSW Group will therefore continue to look at more acquisitions in the years to come, including making a foray into the electric vehicle segment. "Inorganic growth has always been an integral part of our growth journey and we'll continue to explore strategic opportunities, both in the domestic and international markets," said Sajjan Jindal in another interview with *Fortune India* in 2019.

He had recently unveiled plans to invest about $65 billion over the next seven years in the Indian infrastructure sector. In an interview with *The Financial Times* in April 2023, Jindal said that the JSW Group would diversify into new sectors like defence and electric vehicles. The new investment plan—more than double the amount the group had invested in the last ten years—was to be funded by its internal cash, and the sale of shares. JSW would also borrow to help fund expansion into renewable energy, as the group planned to be the least leveraged company within the energy space, Jindal said.

Jindal, who built his empire from virtually zero, is dreaming big. From a company which had to seek debt restructuring in 2002, the group has expanded into new spheres and made its presence felt across the Indian corporate sector.

From a company which had to seek debt restructuring in 2002, the group has expanded into new spheres and made its presence felt across the Indian corporate sector.

"Sajjan Jindal has created a track record of executing large capital-intensive, technically complex, and state-of-the-art steel manufacturing facilities on principles of cost efficiency and operational excellence. He is now making a fast transition to renewable energy... Earning the sobriquet of 'Man of Steel', Sajjan Jindal was the first representative from India to serve as the Chairman of the World Steel Association," consultancy firm EY said while announcing Jindal as the winner of the EY Entrepreneur of the Year™ Award 2022 for scaling the global conglomerate with presence in varied sectors to revenues of US$22 billion, employing over 40,000 people globally.

As the world celebrates Jindal as an entrepreneur, the contribution of the Indian lenders in giving a helping hand to his group at its most vulnerable time must not be forgotten either.

CITATION

Thomas, Prince Matthews. "Sajjan Jindal's Cloning Factory." *Forbes India*, 26 Oct. 2009, www.forbesindia. com/article/big-bet/sajjan-jindals-cloning-factory/6272/1

2.

TATA STEEL

India Inc's Turnaround Specialist

In the early 1990s, Tata Steel—with its eighty-year-old steelmaking plant at Jamshedpur in the eastern Indian state of Bihar (now part of Jharkhand state)—was at a crossroads. There was a brand-new management at Tata Sons, the holding company of the Tata group, with Ratan Tata being the newly appointed chairman. The management was brainstorming ways to transform the laidback company into a global steel enterprise. There was resistance both from within and outside.

"If we do not transform soon, then we will have to turn the plant into a museum and make money by selling tickets," Tata was warned as he took over from the legendary Tata group chairman, JRD "Jeh" Tata in 1991.

In the 32 years since Ratan Tata took over, Tata Steel has witnessed unprecedented transformation from an India-based small steel company to a global steel behemoth.

In the 32 years since Ratan Tata took over, Tata Steel has witnessed unprecedented transformation from an India-based small steel company to a global steel behemoth with huge manufacturing facilities in the United Kingdom and the Netherlands, and with an annual steel production capacity of 35 million tonnes per annum (MTPA).

TV Narendran, a Tata Steel veteran and now the CEO & MD of the company, says that soon after the economic liberalization initiated by then Prime Minister PV Narasimha Rao and Finance Minister Dr. Manmohan Singh, the infamous licence raj was abolished in 1991. Tata Steel, with its limited capacity and older technology, had to face competition for the first time ever.

"Licence raj" is a term coined to depict the Soviet-style strict governmental control and regulation of the Indian economy that was in place after the British left India in 1947, up until 1991.

As per this stifling system, Indian companies were required to apply for licences from the government to operate, to export and import, to buy technology, to sign agreements with foreign partners, etc. Governmental control delayed several projects even as consumers waited for years to receive their deliveries of new products like scooters, cars, and gas cylinders. The liberalization of the Indian economy, after decades of licence raj, ushered in a drastically different era.

"The early '90s was a very challenging period for Tata Steel," says Narendran in an interview in the spring of 2023, at Bombay House—the headquarters of Tata Group. "Until 1991, steel couldn't be imported, as customs duty was very high. Till then, Tata Steel couldn't grow because we needed a licence to expand capacity, which was a very long drawn bureaucratic process. Whether a company wanted to grow or modernize, a licence was needed. When people say that in its 80 years Tata Steel couldn't grow beyond two million tonnes till the '90s, then it was not because we did not have the ambition, but there were too many impediments including the business environment. In the 1990s, we had to adapt very fast and that was a very challenging time, which was ably led by Dr. JJ Irani," says Narendran.

This was also the time when Tata Steel needed the support of its unions, as the company reduced its workforce by half—from around 80,000 to 40,000 in a decade. The Tata group, as was its tradition, offered an extremely generous separation package to its employees for the retirement scheme. "We undertook such a large-scale reduction in workforce without any industrial strife—which is a tribute to the maturity of the management, and the leadership of both the management and the unions at that time," Narendran says.

During this crucial period, several management consultants had even advised Tata to exit the steel business, as competition was too hot to handle for the company. At the same time, Tata Steel was advised to sell its iron ore mining business. But Tata decided to ignore this advice, and instead bet on its people, and on modernizing its operations.

> Tata Steel was advised to sell its iron ore mining business. But Tata decided to ignore this advice, and instead bet on its people, and on modernizing its operations.

The turbulent 1990s was spent on building the foundations for the Tata Steel of today—a progressive global company which is always ready for a new paradigm. The time was used not just in improving employee productivity, but also in investing in the latest facilities for its plants, with modern technologies. "We had programs called modernization of the mind, apart from modernization of the plant. Till the early '90s, steel was rationed, and hence bringing a customer orientation in the organization, and growing the international business were our main initiatives," recalls Narendran.

These initiatives helped move Tata Steel, whose future looked in doubt in the early 1990s, to becoming the lowest cost producer of steel by the end of that decade.

In an event to give away the excellence in quality award to

Tata Steel—among all Tata group companies—Chairman Ratan Tata remarked how Tata Steel would have been the last company in the Tata group to win the quality award. Therefore, this achievement demonstrated the company's ability to transform itself, and the ability of its leadership and its employees to come together to help with this metamorphosis of the company.

"No transformation can be done just by a leader wishing for the transformation of the company. A leader has a role to articulate, communicate, align with the goals. What is special about Tata Steel is that in any kind of crisis, everyone, including the employees, the union, and the management, comes together to resolve the challenges," Narendran notes.

THE 1990S: TRYING TIMES FOR TATA STEEL

When Ratan Tata took over as Tata Sons' chairman in 1991, he faced opposition from several Tata group leaders who had been appointed by JRD Tata. Tata Steel was led by "Russi" Mody—a veteran of 50 years in the company— who rose to become its chairman. The younger Tata was not welcomed by the old Tata hands who resisted changes to the group.

The fight between the old guard and the new ignited with Ratan Tata introducing a retirement policy for all Tata group directors—they were to compulsorily retire at the age of 75. Mody, who was 74 in April 1992, was among several Tata group old-timers including Darbari Seth, SR Vakil, SA Sabavala, Jamshed Bhabha, Nani Palkhivala and JE Talaulicar, who were staring at retirement.

This move did not go well with Mody, who decided to muster support from the Indian financial institutions who owned 48 per cent stake in Tata Steel at that time, while Tata Sons held a minority stake.

According to a report in India Today, in November 1991 Mody decided to appoint his protégé, Aditya Kashyap, to a position just below managing director JJ Irani, without consulting Tata Steel's board of directors. Irani, who was then joint managing director and a Ratan Tata loyalist, shot off a letter of protest to Mody on December 10, 1991, complaining that a "most effective team has been humiliated." Ratan Tata fully supported JJ Irani in the power struggle; battle lines were drawn between Tata and Mody.

Rustomji Homusji Mody had joined Tata Steel in 1939 at the age of 21. He rose through the ranks to become its chairman, with full support from JRD Tata. He was one among many Tata group employees who had been handpicked by JRD to take the company forward. An ageing JRD was fond of his team A; he demonstrated his belief in them by making these professional managers the chairmen of their respective companies. They had all been given a free hand in running the day-to-day operations of the companies.

Consequently, the revolt by Mody surprised JRD who had appointed Ratan Tata as his successor; JRD decided to take up the cudgels on his behalf. JRD met with Prime Minister Narasimha Rao and Finance Minister Manmohan Singh, seeking the government's support in ousting Mody. Mody, on the other hand, met with Bihar Chief Minister Laloo Prasad Yadav and West Bengal Chief Minister Jyoti Basu, to drum up support. The public fight between Tata group's top management now began to take its toll on the performance of the company.

Tata joined hands with "corporate samurai" Nusli Wadia, chairman of the Wadia group of companies, to eject Mody— they took help from several Congress leaders towards this end. In March 1993, Mody was removed from Tata Steel's board, and Ratan Tata was appointed its chairman. A new management structure was finally in place; the company was set for a major transformation under Tata and Irani.

Soon after taking control of the management, a culture of continuous quality upgrade was built by Dr. Irani, who had visited Japan to learn about the TQM (total quality management) journey of Japanese companies. Dr. Irani had gone as part of the Confederation of Indian Industry delegation and, along with other industrialists including Venu Srinivasan of the TVS group, became early proponents of the TQM journey among Indian companies, who were just waking up to global competition.

With Dr. Irani driving the company, TQM implementation became a part of Tata Steel's culture; the company strived for continuous improvement and benchmarking. The ingredients of transformation in company culture were seeded at that time, which helped Tata Steel make huge strides forward, despite several new entrants in the industry.

Tata Steel has had a long history of being written off.

Tata Steel has had a long history of being written off. When the Tata Steel plant was first conceptualized by Jamsetji Tata, the British laughed at the idea, saying that Indians could not make steel. A famous story often quoted in Tata circles is a remark by Sir Frederick Upcott, the chief commissioner of the Great Indian Peninsular Railway, who promised to "eat every pound of steel" that the Tatas succeeded in making. Despite naysayers like Upcott, the first ingot of steel rolled out of the Jamshedpur plant's production line in 1912. But by then, the founder Jamsetji Tata was dead; the project succeeded to see the light of day due to the leadership of his son Dorab, and cousin RD Tata.

Similarly, in the 1990s when the economy was opened up, analysts predicted that new nimble and agile players would come into the industry, and Tata Steel would die. "Every time, Tata Steel transformed itself and came out stronger, which is now a part of the ethos and culture of the company," remarks Narendran, who joined Tata Steel's Jamshedpur plant in 1988, and later moved to the Dubai office to look after their international business. In 1997, Narendran returned to India and was part of the transformation programs—including the supply chain transformation.

"Many times, people underestimated the ability of Tata Steel to transform, and this (negativity) still continues; it's nothing new for us... In the 1990s, the modernization was to cost ₹800 crore which was five or six times of the company's annual profits. Tata Steel had only one option to transform, just before the economy opened up for competition... (Similarly,) soon after World War one, Tata Steel was close to death due to disruptions across the world. But the company kept making spectacular comebacks," Narendran asserts.

Apart from challenges, the 1990s also opened up opportunities for the company. Demand for steel was rising, and imports were turning out to be a big threat to domestic companies. The company had to increase its production to meet the demand, and this ability was built in that decade even as Ratan Tata took full control of the management.

By the end of the decade, Tata Steel was ready for bigger challenges, including the rise of entrepreneur Lakshmi Niwas Mittal.

By the end of the decade, Tata Steel was ready for bigger challenges, including the rise of entrepreneur Lakshmi Niwas Mittal, who left India in 1976 to set up a small steel plant in Indonesia. Mittal aggressively acquired steel plants across the globe, and ended up becoming one of the world's biggest steelmakers by 2006. Tata Steel was far, far behind in global league tables.

THE ACQUISITION STRATEGY

The rise of a local boy to become the world's second-biggest steelmaker was a new challenge for Ratan Tata and his team. Despite being nearly a century old, Tata Steel was not in the club of global steel companies. In 2006, Arcelor— Europe's largest steelmaker—merged with Mittal Steel and came to be called ArcelorMittal. The company had an annual capacity of 88 MTPA. The Tata Steel leadership was often asked by media why they had missed the bus to become a global company like Mittal's. After all, Lakshmi

Mittal had started with virtually nothing. Time was clearly running out for the company.

The company had already built a strong foundation in India in the '90s; it now started looking for acquisitions across the world. The first decade of the millennium was all about growth, and Tata Steel pursued expansion like the rest of the steel industry. It acquired coal and iron ore mines all over the world for raw material security. This was also the decade when China started growing in a big way, and steel consumption went up after it joined the WTO.

The company got ready for growth in India by planning a new steel plant at Kalinganagar in the eastern Indian state of Odisha. In January 2006, when the construction of the wall for the plant was going on, locals protested against the blocking of their cattle grazing routes. Subsequently, violent clashes broke out between the villagers and the police, with the latter firing on protestors. Fourteen people lost their lives in this incident and the ambitious project went into cold storage.

This was also the time when several governments across the world were getting out of steel, as they did not see a strategic need to stay invested in it. The privatization started in Latin America and then spread to Europe. Lakshmi Mittal saw an opportunity here, and started acquiring many of these companies.

> The industry soon realized the importance of
> scale, and the acquisition route was considered
> as the best way to increase capacity, swiftly.

The industry soon realized the importance of scale, and the acquisition route was considered as the best way to increase capacity, swiftly. Until then, the industry had grown via organic means, where it usually took a minimum of three or four years to build a steel plant, and then to expand capacity up to three or four million tonnes. Now, both Mittal and Arcelor were growing via acquisitions. Tata Steel was profitable, but its ranking among global steel companies was at a distant 55th, with a production of four million tonnes. Meanwhile, Arcelor and Mittal Steel were at 50-60 million tonnes of capacity, each.

Their scale would give a competitive edge to companies during procurement of coal, iron ore, and other raw materials. When a rival company bought raw materials at 10 to 20 times the amount at Tata Steel, it then enjoyed a competitive advantage. Tata Steel had signed MoUs to set up steel plants in Odisha, Chhattisgarh, and Jharkhand. The state governments gave iron ore allotments—provided 25 per cent of the capital expenditure were already invested in the state.

For Tata Steel, the decade of the 2000s was more about an increase in input costs and increasing size, as scale became important. But the Kalinganagar firing incident changed the company's thinking—for two years, there was no progress at the site. There was a feeling in Bombay House, the headquarters of the Tata group, that if it were to only depend on growth in India, then it would be too slow to make it to the top leagues. And so, it needed to look at opportunities overseas.

The company zeroed in on NatSteel. Culturally, NatSteel looked like a good match as the company had a footprint across many countries in Southeast Asia. Tata acquired NatSteel in August 2004. A year later, in December 2005, it acquired Millennium Steel in Thailand for $404 million. Then, in January 2007, Tata Steel stunned Corporate India as it acquired Corus Group—a European steel company— for $12 billion, in one of the biggest acquisitions by any Indian company overseas. The acquisition catapulted Tata Steel from its 55th rank to one of the top 10 steelmakers in the world.

At the time of this acquisition, Tata Steel was Asia's first and India's largest integrated private sector steel company, with revenues of $5 billion in 2005-06, and crude steel production of 5 MTPA across India and Southeast Asia. On the other hand, Corus Group was Europe's second largest steel producer with revenues in 2005 of $18 billion and crude steel production of 18.2 MTPA, primarily in the UK and the Netherlands. Corus had 41,100 employees in over

40 countries when Tata Steel acquired the company in an auction.

The combination of Tata Steel—a vertically integrated steel producer and one of the world's most profitable steel companies, with an established and growing presence in India, Southeast Asia and the Pacific-rim countries—and Corus—Europe's second largest steel producer, with a high value-added product range and strong positions in automotive, construction, and packaging—created the world's second most widely spread global steel producer, with a combined presence in 45 countries.

Ratan Tata, Chairman of Tata Steel and Corus, was quoted as saying, "The completion of this acquisition of Corus by Tata Steel is a major step forward in the company's global strategy, and represents an exciting future for both businesses."

Even as the group was celebrating its success in becoming the world's tenth largest steel company, the Lehman crisis hit the world economy.

> As the group was celebrating its success in becoming the world's tenth largest steel company, the Lehman crisis hit the world economy.

The Lehman crisis refers to the bankruptcy of US-based financial services firm, Lehman Brothers, on September

15, 2008. The bankruptcy was the final chapter of the bad loans disbursed by the US banks in the country's real estate sector. After Lehman was notified of a pending credit downgrade due to its heavy position in real estate sector bad loans, the American Federal Reserve summoned several banks to negotiate financing for its reorganization. These discussions failed and Lehman Brothers had to file for bankruptcy—the largest so far in the US, involving more than US$600 billion in assets.

The Lehman bankruptcy triggered a 4.5 per cent one-day drop in the US stock market benchmark index, Dow Jones—then its largest decline since the September 11, 2001 attacks. It signalled a limit to the government's ability to manage the crisis, and spread panic in the financial sector. The entire world economy went into a tailspin following the Lehman crisis with stock markets and commodity prices falling significantly.

THE 2008 CRISIS AND ITS AFTERMATH

The 2008 crisis led to a sharp fall in steel prices which, in turn, led to weaker steel assets losing money. Structurally, the weakest asset in the Tata Steel group was in Europe. The former Corus group's steel plants started bleeding money, and Tata Steel's largest acquisition was gradually becoming an albatross around its neck.

> By 2012, the Tata group also saw a change at
> the top, with Ratan Tata making way for his
> successor, Cyrus Mistry, as the Chairman of the
> group.

By 2012, the Tata group also saw a change at the top, with Ratan Tata making way for his successor, Cyrus Mistry, as the Chairman of the group.

After 2010, Tata Steel made some headway with the local communities and work had started at the construction of the Odisha plant. The Jamshedpur plant capacity, meanwhile, had gone up from 4 million to 7 million tonnes, and by 2014, the capacity was further increased to 9.7 MTPA. The company also looked into the acquisition of Ispat Steel's Dolvi plant, but the race was won by JSW Steel, which was more aggressive in its offer to the lenders.

The focus of the management now was to finish the Kalinganagar project—which had started in 2005 and then lain in cold storage for a few years—and at the same time, to look for more acquisition opportunities.

In 2016, the Indian government enacted the new bankruptcy code which aimed to send loan-defaulting companies to the National Company Law Tribunal for debt resolution. According to the IBC, the defaulting company was auctioned to the highest bidder. That same year, in October 2016, a bitter corporate battle broke out between

Mistry and group patriarch Ratan Tata, as the Tata Sons' board removed Mistry, citing incompetence.

Mistry hit back, accusing Tata of saddling Tata Steel with Corus Group which, he said in a letter to the board of Tata Sons and to the trustees of Tata Trusts, would lead to a write-down of $10 billion for Tata Steel. By January 2017, the Tata group announced that N Chandrasekaran—the former MD and CEO of India's biggest software exporter, TCS—would be the new Chairman of the Tata group. Chandra, as he was popularly known, had his work cut out to bring the Tata group back on track.

In 2017, following the RBI's directions, lenders came out with a list of the top 12 loan defaulters, called the "dirty dozen". Of these, the majority of companies were in the steel industry. This gave an opportunity for cash rich companies to expand their capacity by acquiring one or more of these insolvent companies, to increase their market share and reach.

Several companies including Tata Steel made offers for Electrosteel Steels—which had a 2.5 MTPA steel plant in Jharkhand. Vedanta Limited, a company owned by Anil Agarwal who made his fortune in the metal industry, won the race to acquire Electrosteel Steels.

The company did its due diligence on Bhushan Steel, which was the largest manufacturer of auto-grade steel in India, and also had a 5.6 MTPA steel plant in Odisha. Tata Steel made an aggressive bid of ₹35,200 crore for the company. This was a blockbuster acquisition and was considered a big win for the government's efforts to make the newly enacted bankruptcy code a success. In May 2018, the NCLT approved the acquisition of Bhushan Steel by Tata Steel.

The Bhushan acquisition was much-awaited good news for the Tata group. It had just come out of a bruising corporate war with its former Chairman, Cyrus Mistry. The performance of group chairman N Chandrasekaran and his team was under the microscope and so, the acquisition cleared the atmosphere at Bombay House. It would also make Tata Steel regain its number one position in capacity in the steel sector in India, which it had lost to JSW Steel in recent years.

> The acquisition of Bhushan Steel was a feather in its cap for Tata group, as they won the race after prolonged litigation, and against formidable rivals like JSW Steel and ArcelorMittal.

The acquisition of Bhushan Steel was a feather in its cap for Tata group, as they won the race after prolonged litigation, and against formidable rivals like JSW Steel and ArcelorMittal. Post-acquisition, Tata Steel with its lower cost loans was to reduce the finance cost of Bhushan Steel by half, thus making its turnaround easier.

While the Tatas were busy acquiring Bhushan Steel, the Jhavars of Usha Martin group were in talks with Tata Steel to sell their 1 MTPA long products steel plant in Jamshedpur. By September 2018, Tata Steel signed a definitive agreement with Usha Martin to acquire its steel business, a functional iron ore mine, a coal mine under development, and captive power plants for ₹4,100 crore.

The government was also planning to sell its stake in Neelachal Ispat Nigam Limited, a 1 MTPA steel plant in Odisha, situated right next to Tata Steel's Kalinganagar plant. Since Tata Steel had a bitter experience in acquiring land for its Kalinganagar facility, Neelachal with its 2,500 acres of land would be providential. After the Neelachal acquisition at ₹12,100 crore, Tata Steel, along with its own facilities, had access to 6,000 acres of land for future expansion of as high as 25 MTPA. As a bonus, Neelachal had iron ore mines to produce steel.

THE TURNAROUNDS

When Tata acquired Bhushan Steel, the plant was producing around 2.9 MTPA; by mid-2023, it was producing 5 MTPA of steel. The company soon became debt-free and it was finally merged with Tata Steel. Tata Steel paid up to ₹18,000 crore of debt in lieu of Bhushan Steel to the banks. In the case of Usha Martin too, the company repaid its loans and merged it with Tata Sponge (the erstwhile Tata Steel Long Products), now merged with Tata Steel.

The management delivered all the numbers which it had promised at the time of acquisition. "As a consequence, Tata Steel as an organization acquired great confidence in its ability to adapt and transform itself. While we had decent success in NatSteel and Tata Steel Thailand, and the Corus Group had its own set of problems, there was a feeling (of doubt about) whether we can acquire companies and then turn them around. I think with all these acquisitions, we've proved to ourselves and grown in confidence," says Narendran.

"I think that confidence has grown with each of these assets. People are more willing to volunteer for turnaround jobs, go there and fix it, and there's a lot of pride associated with being in the turnaround team," Narendran beams.

"The team which had done the due diligence did a fantastic job. The Neelachal plant was like a forest, as the plant was closed for three years. To start producing at full capacity within 12 months was a big achievement," he says.

$$\infty$$

Narendran recalls his first look at Neelachal when they went around the plant for due diligence. "It was a sense of déjà vu. Tata Steel had acquired a 100-year old company in

Jamshedpur called Indian Steel & Wire Products under the BIFR, in 2004. The factory had a forest growing inside, the roofs had caved in, and machines were rusted. The factory was in terrible condition but within six months, the clean-up happened and soon it was back in action."

However, the Tata Steel team knew that Neelachal was in much better shape than it seemed. "We had done our due diligence beforehand, and we knew that the blast furnace and the steel mill shop were not bad. We knew we could run the plant. We had taken our teams and since we had Kalinganagar next door, our existing team was involved," Narendran adds.

"We did not want to lose the asset, and we were confident that we could fix things and turn it around. The biggest challenge will be the coke plant which will take at least a year to restart, but the rest of the facilities could start really fast. When we acquired the asset, we promised to restart the plant within 100 days, and we started producing steel on time," he says. The coke plant was commissioned in August 2023.

PICKING THE RIGHT TEAM

One of the cornerstones to turning around the facilities at Bhushan Steel and at Neelachal was to put together the right team. As Narendran notes, "We built the team with the right mix of people with a good blend of youth and experienced people, apart from having a team with different operational capabilities. In Neelachal, we sent one of our very senior maintenance people, and the other person had rich experience in running the blast furnaces. This was a fantastic opportunity for learning for everyone."

Bhushan Steel was a good production facility, but it had been poorly run. Due to lack of funds, the earlier management had cut the budget for maintenance. Poor maintenance, in turn, led to unpredictable operating performance. The company had not paid its vendors or its employees. "We were very confident that we could increase the capacity of this plant to 5 million tonnes from 3 million tonnes, without making a large investment," Narendran says.

In fact, when Bhushan Steel was being built, its erstwhile promoters—the Singhal family—had visited the Tata Steel plant and built an identical blast furnace with help from Tata's suppliers. Hence, the Tata Steel management knew what was in store for them at Bhushan Steel in Odisha. After the acquisition, the 3 MTPA plant was soon increased to 5 MTPA; investments were made to fix everything and get the plant restarted.

While Bhushan was a good and newly built plant, Usha Martin was partly old and partly new, but it had a good culture of producing very high quality steel. Neelachal was not a bad plant, but was not run efficiently. Its equipment—

including the blast furnace and the steel mill shop—were good, but they had not been run at all. The people, the equipment, the culture, procurement practices and human resource processes—these were different in all three companies, which created different kinds of challenges for the new management.

"It's very important to send the right people from the beginning. We handpicked 30-40 people from Tata Steel and sent them to these three companies. We had already identified the weak areas in all three plants. We had identified the people at the target company who would fit in with our culture. For example, if we knew that the steel mill shop required more experienced people, then we sent people from Tata Steel," Narendran explains.

The Tata Steel team was briefed to be humble and not to throw their weight around. In many processes, the team was told, the target company may have better practices; so members should go with the humility to learn from them, and to share from Tata Steel's experiences. However, there were some non-negotiables across the companies: Safety, Environment, and Ethics. Some people who could not make the cut on the ethics front were asked to leave, so that the message went out to all. There was absolutely no mandate to go and sack people, but some people left when they figured they couldn't fit in with Tata values.

Tata Steel sent senior people from its management to look after all three plants.

At Neelachal, more than 90 per cent of the team was retained, while the remainder was sent from Tata Steel. One of the first tasks here was to pay pending salaries for the last two years to Neelachal employees. This helped to get the 1,300 employees on board with the new management. The Tata management provided buses to pick up people from their homes, canteens were spruced up, and the new management started living in the NINL colony.

In Bhushan, too, the Tata Steel management team spent their time at the plants across India. Integration of the Usha Martin plant was a lot easier as it was in Jamshedpur.

"You have to get the buy-in of the people and set clear boundary conditions on what is acceptable and what is not acceptable. We have to be very clear what we are trying to chase. We have to get the right people and have the respect of and for the local team, and make them feel part of the change," Narendran advises.

SORTING TECHNOLOGICAL MISMATCHES

The technology used by Bhushan Steel was like any other flat products plant of Tata Steel, so there was not much difference in plant equipment. On the other hand, Usha Martin was still using an old mill of Tata Steel, which they had acquired from the secondhand market in the

1990s. Once Tata Steel took over, Usha Martin's plant was upgraded to a newer version to manufacture steel. At NINL, the facilities were good to go and ready for expansion.

The technology mismatch, however, was more glaring in their software, as all four companies—Tata Steel, Bhushan, Neelachal and Usha Martin—were using different technology to produce steel.

All three of the acquired companies had underinvested in technology. This turned out to be a big part of Tata Steel's planning and expenditure. To integrate Tata Steel with the others, it implemented the SAP system with Bhushan Steel, which was using an older version. But what surprised the Tata brass was that Neelachal didn't have computers; it was using a very basic Enterprise Resource Planning (ERP) system. The very day Tata Steel acquired NINL, it implemented the SAP system and integrated it with Tata Steel's systems. The company started training Neelachal staff two months before the actual takeover, so that integration would be smooth right from day one.

INTEGRATING PROCUREMENTS AND BANK DEALINGS

Soon after their acquisitions, the procurement departments of the three companies plugged into the larger Tata Steel ecosystem, to get better terms from suppliers. The combined procurement of raw materials and other materials gave several synergistic benefits to the companies. Tata Steel bought 40 million tonnes of raw materials like iron ore and coal pellets from a number of suppliers across the world for its manufacturing units in India, the Netherlands, and the UK. Tata Steel, the Indian entity, also had a captive production of 40 million tonnes comprising its own iron ore, coking coal, and other commodities like chrome and manganese ore. Therefore these companies, which were buying a much smaller volume, could benefit from synergies of scale with Tata Steel, receiving better payment terms, better technical assessments of blends, etc. This helped handle raw materials better, operationally, as well as to reduce the raw material cost.

There was also a lot of leakage from these companies—either due to malpractices, related party transactions, or other vested interests. Tata Steel started a clean-up of procurement practices and renegotiated several contracts. For example, Bhushan Steel was paying a huge rent of ₹6 crore a month for its office in New Delhi. The office was immediately shut down and the staff was transferred to either the Tata Steel office in Delhi, or asked to work from the Sahibabad plant in Uttar Pradesh, 35 kilometres east of the capital city.

Several contracts, which were paid for by the erstwhile management at higher rates, were renegotiated, and thus unlocked value for Tata Steel.

Tata Steel's central team for procurement, now known as Group Strategic Procurement, operates out of Singapore and has staff in the Netherlands and the UK too; they work together as one team to make big ticket purchases.

While local sites are authorized to make decisions on smaller-sized purchases, the group is always looking at opportunities to make common purchasing decisions for all sites. Teams from all sites are sent to other countries for making joint purchase decisions for smaller items, to get benefits during negotiations. Hence, when there is an advantage to making purchases by the central team, then the company buys it centrally; but when there's an advantage in buying from local sources, then the local team is authorized to make the purchase. The idea is to find a balance between agility and scale, and to make sure every buck is saved by the holding company and its subsidiaries, while ensuring quality too.

> The idea is to find a balance between agility and scale, and to make sure every buck is saved by the holding company and its subsidiaries, while ensuring quality too.

Another measure which helped the Tata Steel top brass to turnaround companies was to integrate treasuries and bank dealings. For instance, when Bhushan Steel was raising funds, its borrowing costs were far higher than at Tata Steel—which is a much better rated company. As Tata Steel merges all its listed subsidiaries with itself, the benefits of synergy will trickle down to all its companies.

Tata Steel in India grew in just one decade from 9 MTPA to 21 MTPA (by fiscal 2023), mainly via the M&A route and the commissioning of a new plant at Kalinganagar. Going forward, Tata Steel Kalinganagar will expand from 3 MTPA to 8 MTPA; it could even expand to 16 MTPA with its land bank. The Bhushan Steel site is to be expanded from 5.6 MTPA and has the potential to go up to 10 MTPA. The Neelachal site also has the potential of expansion from 1 MTPA to 10 MTPA, in stages. With the existing plan, the company can increase its capacity to 50 MTPA. Of this, the company is targeting 40 million tonne capacity by 2030.

The long term idea of Tata Steel is to have fewer sites with larger volumes, rather than several steel producing sites with lower capacity. With the emergence of global giants like ArcelorMittal and JSW, steel markets have become a very competitive environment. Tata Steel plans to have a capacity of at least 10 to 15 MTPA at each of its sites.

NO SINGULAR STRATEGY FOR TURNAROUNDS

Narendran says that while acquiring and turning around each company, Tata did not follow a one-size-fits-all approach. Just because something works in one place, doesn't mean it would work everywhere. The fundamentals come down to assessing the situation in terms of the facilities, the people, the context, the market, and the gaps. The CEO has to be deeply involved in that assessment. "For me, personally, it was important to see those sites and spend time and get a feel. This is much deeper than reading a report which somebody has given. The CEO must get a feel for the place, the culture of the place, the facilities," Narendran suggests for future generations of leaders.

The fundamentals come down to assessing the situation in terms of the facilities, the people, the context, the market, and the gaps.

For example, during the Neelachal visit, the Tata Steel team led by Narendran met the local staff and checked the facilities to plan their priorities. "We realized that we have to first change the roof, clean up the shrubbery, and get a feel of areas that need to be fixed. The rest of the team will (then) look into the facilities more closely. For example, the coke plant head at Tata Steel will have a close look at the coke plant and decide the priorities. Similarly, the blast furnace expert from Tata Steel will look at the condition of the target company's blast furnace. Later, at the team meeting, every team head will detail their priorities and concerns. The targets will be set for every department on when they can get the plant started."

The CEO will need to know exactly where the issues are. "I think the CEO has to be deeply involved and get his own feel for the acquisition, as ultimately, if I have to go and convince my board about the acquisition, then first I have to be convinced," Narendran says.

Another important thing is to pick and deploy the right people for turning around an asset. "If you send the wrong people, then anything can go wrong and even a good asset can go wrong. Tata Steel will send only a fraction of its people to run a plant, and that team has to be a good bridge between Tata Steel and the company. Our people are the ambassadors of Tata Steel... they must have the maturity to be good ambassadors, and should deal with the anxieties and the issues of the local people," Narendran says.

For employees at newly acquired sites, there's a sweeping cultural change.

For employees at newly acquired sites, there's a sweeping cultural change. If you want to change the culture, then you have to tell them about the new culture, and why it matters. "Sending the right people and setting very clear goals for them is very important for a successful turnaround," he insists.

Tata Steel's internal due diligence team visits the sites, and brainstorms on these projects. The team assesses the progress of newly acquired assets, and eventually the savings are scrutinized by Tata Steel's own audit team.

The code word for Bhushan Steel was B1. Once the acquisition was complete, the B1 code was changed to 'Be One' meaning that it aimed to become number one. Since Bhushan and Usha Martin have already been integrated with Tata Steel, the top management now gets weekly MIS (Management Information Systems) reports of Neelachal alone, so as to keep tabs on its sales and production. During the initial integration, Tata Steel management closely monitored the other companies too, but later, things were left to the local management.

Tata Steel had also invited group Chairman, N Chandrasekaran, and other independent directors, to visit the new sites. The interaction with the top management motivates workers at the new plants to do better and also makes them feel like a part of the Tata family. "Of course, there are many issues, and everything isn't nice and perfect. Sometimes people get upset over changes in designations during the integration. Tata Steel has a conservative designation practice and that may upset new employees," Narendran says.

"Having a good sense of the context, sending the right people, setting the right goals, celebrating the successes, being very clear on the culture and the goals, and building the right IT systems are fundamentals for any turnaround," Narendran sums up.

Closing the deal is easy, but the transformation of an acquired entity is a big challenge. Once the team is calibrated and all the basic stuff is fixed, then it becomes like any other site.

As steel is a cyclical industry, everyone does well during the good times, but how companies survive the down cycle is what's important. In the 30 years since liberalization, several companies decided to set up steel plants in India, but not many of them survived once steel prices dropped.

Take, for instance, Bhushan Steel. Once a Tata Steel customer, Bhushan Steel used to buy hot rolled coils for its UP plant, and always paid on time. The company was cash rich and debt free. But when steel prices went up in 2000,

Neeraj Singhal decided to set up a steel plant, which turned out to be his downfall. There were also external issues with Bhushan Steel that contributed to their troubles. The company lost its coal mines, and an accident led to the closure of its plant.

DVR Seshadri, a professor at ISB, credits Tata Steel's successful turnarounds to the hands-on approach of the top management, where quality was anchored at the level of the CEO. "The belief was that quality and cost reinforce each other: pushing for higher quality would result in lowering the cost of production. Rather than launch improvement initiatives sequentially, the management chose to launch a variety of initiatives in parallel, with the belief: 'Let a thousand flowers bloom.' This enabled each employee to pick and choose those initiatives that resonated with each individual," he says.

Having put the spotlight on quality, a comprehensive approach was taken, focusing on the calibre of every aspect of functioning of the organization, rather than a narrowed focus on product quality alone. The next big leap was to move from quality to business excellence. The US-based Malcolm Baldridge performance excellence model was adapted, and named the 'The Tata Business model.' An aspirational score of 600 on a total possible score of 1000 was set, and mechanisms were put in place to rapidly achieve this target.

Over the years, the company has continued to improve on this performance scale each year. Through the rollout of the Balanced Scorecard, accountability was instilled at every level in the organization, starting from the top.

The focus then shifted to competency-building at every stage, with a view to making the company a perpetual 'learning organization'. Focus on the customer was intensified. An audacious vision was co-created through an elaborate visioning process that encompassed every employee. Processes were streamlined to eliminate friction. Recognizing that ideas for improvement could emanate from anywhere in the organization, an atmosphere was created to harness ideas stemming from the grassroots.

A key factor to success was that the implementation was owned by employees of the company, rather than through delegation of this responsibility to consultants. This massive push resulted in the company becoming the lowest cost steel producer in the world.

At the turn of the century, Tata Steel was rated number one by the World Steel Dynamics in terms of quality, delivery reliability and cost. Having achieved this distinction, the next step was to implement similar drastic improvement processes to address the connection with the marketplace, for which a slew of initiatives were rolled out for success in both business-to-business (B2B) and business-to-consumer (B2C) markets.

Having scaled great heights by 2005, which was in sharp contrast to the dismal situation of the company at the time of India's liberalization, the company turned its attention to growth. "It had the financial muscle to embark on several acquisitions. The focus enlarged to develop leadership across the organization, create a global mindset among the employees, while keeping the organization agile. The challenge at this stage was to create an entrepreneurial culture across the organization, to fuel innovation that is less top-driven," Seshadri says.

A massive thrust on digital transformation across the organization enabled the company to be future-fit.

Many of the lessons learnt in the turnaround of operations during 1992-2000, were progressively implemented across other aspects of the company, such as in marketing. A massive thrust on digital transformation across the organization enabled the company to be future-fit. The company successfully transitioned from pure product play to one that took tailored innovative solutions to its various key customer segments. Based on this successful turnaround, the company has become one of the top ten steel producers in the world. (https://worldsteel.org/data/top-producers/)

CITATION

Pathak, Rahul and Ravi, A.B. "Grim Lobbying in Tata-Russi Mody Feud May Decide Tisco's Fate." *India Today*, 15 June 1992. www.indiatoday.in/magazine/economy/story/19920615-grim-lobbying-in-tata-russi-mody-feud-may-decide-tisco-fate-766404-2013-01-08

3.

L&T

How Anil Manibhai Naik Transformed the Indian Conglomerate

n February 2023, then Group Chairman of L&T, Anil Manibhai Naik, boarded an early morning flight to Anand, a town situated 470 kilometres north of Mumbai. Naik, along with his close family members, was to attend a felicitation ceremony organized by his alma mater—Birla Vishvakarma Mahavidyalaya Engineering College.

As Naik walked into the massive makeshift hall in the college playground, thousands of students, faculty members, and residents of Anand broke into thunderous applause to welcome their most successful alumnus. Here was the man who not only made L&T what it is today—a $27 billion conglomerate—but also inspired a generation of young engineers from small towns to dream big. "I was one of the few who were hired by L&T in 1965, even though I did not have a degree from the Indian Institute of Technology. If I can stand here today as L&T's chairman, then any one of you can do it. All you need is the passion to dream big and the willingness to work hard," Naik told the dreamy-eyed students.

The two characteristics—vision and diligence—are often seen as defining features of a leader, and Naik had them both in ample measure. In fact, he had demonstrated them right from his school days in the village of Kharel, just a couple of hundred kilometres from the Anand campus of the engineering college.

Naik, who studied in a Gujarati-medium school, is not your regular high-flying CEO—his background is quite atypical. Born on June 9, 1942, Naik started his schooling in Mumbai at Hansraj Morarji Public School in Andheri; he moved to a village school in south Gujarat after his father was offered a job as the principal. Naik graduated from the college in Anand with a degree in Mechanical Engineering. He worked with Nestor Boilers before joining L&T.

In an interview with the author, Naik recalls the precepts he learnt from his father, a strongly nationalistic school teacher of sterling values. He says, "My father told me to try and get elected as the prefect of the class."

The young Anil Naik followed his father's words to the letter. "Throughout my student life, I contested both going leadership positions—Prefect and General Secretary. In fact, I was a student leader of the college at the age of 21." The experience taught Naik a clutch of valuable lessons that stood him in good stead later in life. Chief among them was the ability to rally people around a cause and motivate them. "That is how I became adept at managing the workers' unions at L&T," says Naik. "I was good at managing people and building a rapport with all of them." At L&T, he is fabled for the kind of people skills which help him both charm his listeners when the occasion called for it, and command them when required.

On graduation, around 90 per cent of his class yielded to the lure of careers in the West at a time when visas were easily available. But young Naik stood his ground. He vowed to stay back in India and help create an organization that would be as good as any in the West. "L&T had always been my dream career destination," he said at the L&T's Annual General Meeting in August 2023, "because it fulfilled my two ambitions—I wanted to join an engineering company, and it had to be an organization that contributes to building the nation. With L&T, both my requirements converged." In an earlier interview with the author, Naik explained, "Even at the age of 20, I could sense that there was hardly any company which could serve the country, other than L&T."

Founded by Danish engineers Henning Holck-Larsen and Søren Kristian Toubro in 1938, the Mumbai-based company commonly known as L&T is now one of the big names in corporate India.

Founded by Danish engineers Henning Holck-Larsen and Søren Kristian Toubro in 1938, the Mumbai-based company commonly known as L&T is now one of the big names in corporate India. It has attracted attention from a range of international investors. Its current shareholders include giant global asset managers BlackRock, Norway's Norges Bank, and the Indian asset management unit of Japan's Nippon Life.

In his early days at L&T, Naik spoke halting English—he was not a product of the IITs or IIMs that produced most CEOs for India Inc., and global companies. He was in that sense an outlier. But Naik proved that if you have the leadership quotient needed, you can achieve success by rising above all obstacles. Swiftly recognizing that English was the lingua franca of business and industry, Naik learnt the language through self-teaching cassettes. He began holding his own among peers in leading companies. Being blessed with a powerful voice and a dominant presence, he soon emerged as a compelling speaker across all forums.

What worked in his favour were his deep domain knowledge, and his capacity for hard work. Long hours every day and all through the week—including Sundays—became routine. Naik reportedly did not take a break for over twenty years of his life. After all, making an Indian multinational company is no easy task.

In 1999, Naik was appointed as L&T's CEO and could look back with a justifiable sense of accomplishment. At every phase of his journey, even as his immediate career objectives modified over the years, one deep underlying ambition stayed unchanged—his desire to transform L&T into a true Indian multinational. In pursuit of that ambition, he has won professional recognition and a host of awards—94 at last count. The array includes high state and national honours such as the Gujarat Garima (2009), the Padma Bhushan (2009), and the Padma Vibhushan (2019).

CHANGE IN THE AIR

In April 1999, when Naik strode into the CEO's office on the first floor of L&T House at Ballard Estate, Mumbai, people both within and outside the company braced themselves for change of a seismic order. It was like the approach of a storm—things would certainly not be the same anymore. As one of his understudies said, "Naik s*aab* had revamped the shop floor when he was in charge. He turned around the businesses that he handled, and made them flagship businesses. Basically, he transforms everything he touches."

At the turn of the century, it was almost as if history paused to see what he would do with the company, now that he was in complete charge. True to form, he brought in unprecedented changes of composition and character, scale and speed. Thus far, the company had been progressing on lines that were fairly predictable. Beginning with trade, it moved into the manufacturing of equipment for dairies and chemical plants. Even at that early stage, it developed a reputation for strong customer service. Years later, Naik would build further upon this platform, to include shareholders and other stakeholders.

'If it's not broken, don't fix it' is a frequently quoted leadership dictum. So why would a new leader feel compelled to change anything in L&T? If you asked that question, you definitely didn't know Naik. In his mind, Naik was clear that his would not be just another episode in the long and storied history of L&T. As he put it bluntly when he talked to his employees, "L&T will have to change." The transformation was drastic and swift—from business contours to work culture. And every bit of it contributed to his dream of building an Indian multinational company.

Naik set himself an immediate agenda—a checklist of tasks that he would complete in his first 90 days as CEO. Each item on his list was impactful. Strange as it may now seem, the concept of value creation was unfamiliar to many in the company back then. They were excellent engineers no doubt, but Naik wanted them to be more—to think like good entrepreneurs. "In anything and everything you do, if you are not constantly creating value, you are missing opportunity and time," he would tell his colleagues.

Naik exposed the rank and file of the company to contemporary, often contrarian, views. It is possible that by comparing themselves to other India-based companies, L&T engineers had been lulled into complacence. Their work culture was almost that of a government organization. So, Naik changed their frame of reference. Being the best in India was not good enough—you had to be as good as your global peers, for the aim was to make L&T a globally benchmarked organization. The age of protected economies was becoming history, and competition was closing in. From being top of the class, L&T suddenly woke up to the fact that there was a lot of catching up for it to do.

> From being top of the class, L&T suddenly woke up to the fact that there was a lot of catching up for it to do.

Naik initiated the process of creating a new vision statement for the company. "It set the compass for the direction which the company would take. It also changed its growth trajectory and its velocity. We also drew up a strategic roadmap which ensured that we periodically re-examine our portfolio through the lens of emerging market realities. It was a comprehensive blueprint for transformation," he remarks.

At first glance, all the goals that he set—creating value, emphasizing the importance of people, rationalizing the portfolio, and going international—were different from one another. Yet they were all interlinked and interdependent. Together they would shield the company against takeover threats in the future.

GETTING OUTSIDE THE ECHO CHAMBER

Old respected companies tend to have one common failing—they dwell in an echo chamber.

Old respected companies tend to have one common failing—they dwell in an echo chamber. When you inhabit the corridors of an organization for too long, you hear only conformist opinions, affirming what is conventionally done. Countering this shortcoming called for deliberate strategy. External speakers suddenly found themselves invited to 'workouts' at L&T. It was here that some home truths were aired. One of the speakers plainly asked the assembled group of senior L&T executives, "Have you seen the trading of your stock? It's lying in one corner. Nobody is interested in your stock, because while they know it's a great company, and it will do great jobs, it has little to offer to the shareholders". Clearly, something had to done, and fast.

While there were external challenges aplenty, another arena lay within L&T's gates—the organization of the company. The company was getting unwieldy and laboured in its response to rapidly changing circumstances. Remedial action came in the form of a revamped organizational structure, which turned the company into sharply focused businesses. This led to greater accountability. Under the glare of a searching review, inadequacies would be out in the open.

Naik began the transformation by putting the building blocks in place—creating the right teams by emphasizing talent, and then expanding their horizons. Naik turned his attention to L&T's Leadership Training Academy at Lonavala, near Mumbai. A modest set-up, he infused the academy with greater ambition. It had to measure up to the responsibility of moulding the future leaders of the company, virtually becoming a corporate university.

A major milestone in Naik's long and eventful journey was the setting up of the world class manufacturing complex in Hazira, near Surat.

A major milestone in Naik's long and eventful journey was the setting up of the world class manufacturing complex in Hazira, near Surat; it is now renamed the A.M. Naik Heavy Engineering Complex. The Complex has been at the forefront of technology created to meet the needs of the country. Incidentally, the company's new soaring corporate office in Powai, Mumbai, also carries the name 'A.M. Naik Towers', in acknowledgement of his seminal contribution to every aspect of L&T's expansion and growth.

"When I visited Hazira for the first time in the 1980s, it was marshy land—only in the low tide could we see the land. I had to wear a gumboot and walk over three kilometres of slush to inspect the land. I acquired 200 acres in Hazira and it shook up the top management at L&T House," Naik recalls. After L&T set up its complex, other industrial houses too set up their units in Hazira, including Reliance Industries and Essar Steel.

"We did several studies on flooding as we wanted to protect our plant even if there were a 'once in a 100 years' type of flooding," says Naik. "When Reliance was setting up its plant in Hazira, they enquired what I had done. When I told them that I had filled five feet, nine inches, their men were instructed to do the same. So Reliance didn't have to do all the studies, and saved their money."

Today, L&T's A.M. Naik Heavy Engineering Complex is a waterfront multi-facility campus dedicated to modular fabrication for offshore and onshore projects, heavy engineering, defence, and power equipment manufacturing facilities. It is equipped to manufacture extra-large and very heavy equipment for power projects, as well as for chemical, refinery, petrochemical, and fertilizer industries.

A policy of periodic review ensures that the facilities remain relevant to changing times and needs. Naik says that since coal-based power plants are now losing market due to environmental concerns, they are shifting focus to manufacturing green hydrogen at the site.

Naik was also instrumental in setting up L&T's IT and IT-related businesses. He was the one who first articulated the IT vision of the company, and then proceeded to nurture it during its formative years. This was the time when several well-established business houses including RPG, the Birla group, the Hindujas, ICICI, and ITC had failed to crack the infotech business, and remained small players in the IT space. For L&T, it was hard going in the initial days. But they had an untiring chairman who stood shoulder to shoulder with sales engineers and ensured that orders turned into 'wins'. The story goes that he would often take overnight flights from Mumbai to New York and meet potential clients at 9 AM in the morning at Manhattan, going straight from the airport to make his pitch.

The seeds sowed in those times continue to bear fruit to this day. "We transformed an internal wing of the parent company into a market-facing, customer-centric organization—now known as LTIMindtree," says Naik. "We also carved out three related businesses from the parent company and formed a stand-alone company—L&T Technology Services (LTTS)." The expertise of LTTS contributed significantly to the Digital India Programme.

L&T has been associated for almost three decades with the defence sector. In a speech to shareholders Naik said, "There are encouraging signals on the defence front... India's journey towards self-reliance or *atmanirbharta* is transitioning from stated intention to visible action. The government is keen to reduce import dependency and go a step further to secure for India an entry into the global supply chain."

In 2019, L&T set up the Armoured Systems Complex (ASC)—a 50-acre greenfield state-of-the-art manufacturing facility in Hazira—to make advanced military armoured platforms like self-propelled Howitzers, air-defence systems, infantry combat vehicles, future-ready combat vehicles and battle tank parts. "We have already delivered 100 howitzer guns to the Indian Army, and in December 2024, we won a further order for an additional 100 guns. The guns are performing extremely well at high altitude in Ladakh, and two regiments are now using them," Naik states.

Another business that Naik conjured out of nowhere for L&T was the real estate business. This turned out to be an instant success.

Another business that Naik conjured out of nowhere for L&T was the real estate business. This turned out to be an instant success—L&T Realty is doing well, despite being a rather late entrant. And while Naik was setting up new businesses, he was also selling others. The marketplace has no room for sentiment. Around 16 businesses were divested by him, since they were out of alignment with the organization's roadmap.

PROTECTING THE COMPANY

When embarking on the turnaround of L&T, Naik had also needed to simultaneously fight another, and bigger, battle—protecting L&T from the corporate raiders who tried to take over the company in the late eighties. "In the latter part of 2001, the unique professional character of L&T was threatened as it faced the imminent possibility of being taken over by a large, family-owned conglomerate," Naik recalled in his speech at the shareholders meeting in 2023. "It took astute leadership to resolve the conflict and achieve a win-win solution that left everyone satisfied."

Naik had fought to the hilt to protect L&T. He had made representations to all concerned to let L&T preserve its professional management culture. It was only after extensive negotiations that a solution was reached which allowed L&T to retain its engineering business. Meanwhile, the Aditya Birla Group, which had amassed 12 per cent stake in L&T, acquired the cement business which L&T had anyhow wanted to exit.

There were other positive outcomes to measures taken at this time—the formation of the employees' foundation now ring-fences L&T against any future takeover attempts. While defending L&T against the takeover, Naik achieved a dramatic volte-face which enabled him to form a unique Employee Trust. This gives L&T employees unprecedented opportunities for medical care, scholarships, and multiple other benefits. The L&T Employee Trust, which is chaired by Naik, is considered a one-of-a-kind achievement in industry. Also, since its formation, the company no longer has the Damocles sword of a takeover hanging overhead.

"I am the founder chairman of the trust that holds 14.2 per cent of equity in L&T, thus making it the single largest shareholder. After I gave stock options to the employees, employee families found they had more money to spend. In a way, this helped me to reduce attrition, as spouses would often tell their husbands not to leave L&T," Naik laughs.

Between 1999, when Naik took over as the CEO, and September 2023, when he retired, the L&T group's revenues grew 37 times: from ₹5,000 crore to nearly ₹1,83,000 crore on a like-to-like basis. This surge, achieved largely through organic growth, has few parallels in corporate India.

In the same period, the market capitalization of L&T (excluding infotech companies) climbed from around ₹4,000 crore to around ₹4.88 trillion (as of January 2023) at a compounded annual growth rate of nearly 20 per cent. This enabled the company to issue bonus shares four times to its shareholders, thus increasing their shareholdings nine times. All this is apart from the generous dividends which they receive every year.

The market valuation of LTIMindtree and other IT-related companies of L&T has gone up from zero to close to ₹2.25 trillion. The acquisition of rival software exporter Mindtree for ₹10,000 crore in 2019 has ramped up Naik's strategy to grow in higher-margin businesses. "We have set up L&T's software services business from zero to become India's fifth-largest software services company," Naik told the author.

"We are expanding software services, data centres, and technology services as we see growth from these businesses. Today, 30 per cent of L&T group's market value comes from the software and engineering services companies," Naik said effusively, speaking from L&T's establishment on Mumbai's Pali Hill. The international thrust that Naik initiated soon after he took over at the helm has also borne fruit. Today over 40% of L&T's revenue comes from international business.

Under Naik, efficiency received a boost when the threshold for L&T's acceptable orders was raised to ₹25 crore and above. Smaller orders took too much management bandwidth and were not considered worth the effort. Over time, the target size for orders was raised to ₹100 crore, and now the company does not, in the normal course, participate in orders below ₹1,000 crore. "The idea was to make more profits, and not focus on small-sized orders which took a lot of time and energy," Naik says. This is most apparent in the construction business.

"Our association with infrastructure goes back over seven decades," says Naik. "But it is only after 2006, when construction began to be more closely integrated with the rest of the company, that we could scale up everything we did. In just 11 years, the infrastructure business grew approximately 20 times, and profits went up 45 times." Given its current market valuation, it is impossible for anyone to make a hostile raid on L&T. Naik's visionary words ring true: "We should perform so well that it should become impossible for anyone to buy shares in our company, because good results will make the stock expensive for acquisition."

SUCCESSION PLANNING

Naik has always been strongly committed to succession planning. He believes professional managers with leadership qualities can add value, whereas entrepreneurial leaders with excellent management skills can multiply value several times over. This was the kind of leader whom Naik set himself to develop.

Like almost every other project that he undertook, Naik decided to raise the bar in succession planning. It wasn't going to be easy, but he kept his eyes open. Finally, he spotted SN Subrahmanyan, an engineer who, as Naik said: "had a spark in him." He was from the infrastructure group; in its entire history, L&T had never had a CEO who emerged from the infrastructure segment. But Naik was undeterred by lack of precedent, and began to actively groom Subrahmanyan for the top job, ignoring conventional rules of seniority and overcoming murmurs of opposition. It was an elaborate process that required a great deal of effort.

Interestingly, Naik does not treat a problem in isolation. He develops a solution, and then institutionalizes it, so that potential problems can be forestalled.

In a calculated move, Naik deputed Subrahmanyan to the US and the UK to familiarize himself with the company's IT-related businesses. This would give the infrastructure professional a much-needed IT orientation. On his return, he was appointed Vice Chairman, followed by the chairmanship of L&T's Hyderabad Metro business, and the Kattupalli Shipyard. It culminated in one of the smoothest top-level succession stories in Indian industry.

Interestingly, Naik does not treat a problem in isolation. He develops a solution, and then institutionalizes it, so that potential problems can be forestalled. He helped to make the leadership pipeline more robust by introducing what is known within the company as the '7 Step Leadership Programme'. This skilfully-devised training programme identifies budding leadership talent, and through a series of interventions, moulds them into business leaders of global calibre. At the sixth step, a select few are offered exposure to top-shelf institutions like Harvard, INSEAD, and Wharton. Those who make it to the seventh and final step are directly mentored by Naik himself.

Incidentally, all the current top management (as of Dec 2024) has been mentored by Naik.

A staunch nationalist, Naik believes that for India to progress, the people at the bottom of the pyramid must flourish. "Almost 80 per cent of the Indian population is below middle class and 40 per cent are below the poverty line. Developing infrastructure should be the top priority... to develop the country and take people out of poverty." Naik is also vocal about the need to encourage philanthropy, and adopt a more inclusive approach to progress. He says, "We cannot have an India for the rich and an India for the rest. Unity amid diversity is to be welcomed. But unity amid disparity is not sustainable."

After stepping down from executive responsibilities, Naik's focus is increasingly on philanthropy. He sees it as part of his larger mission of building the nation. "It's not only the wealthy who can help the disadvantaged", he says. "You don't need a lot of money for philanthropy. All you need is a heart. *Dil chahiye.*" Naik has donated around 75 per cent of his personal wealth to help the disadvantaged. In 2009, he set up two trusts—the Nirali Memorial Medical Trust to channelize his contribution to the healthcare sector, and the AM Naik Charitable Trust to deal with education and skill-building. "Both my Trusts", he says, "are connected to life—one protects life, the other transforms it."

Post-retirement, Naik spends his spare time in informal political analysis. "India is blessed to have a prime minister like Narendra Modi. He works 16 to 17 hours a day and always appears fresh for the meetings. I wonder where India would have gone if Modi was not there," Naik says in his no-nonsense manner. "Since 2014—when he came to power—we have accelerated the core sector work of the country... We have enhanced our defence capabilities and boosted our energy reserves. So in all respects, be it our banking system, our adoption of digital India, implementation of 5G technology in telecom, we are right there, on par with the Europeans and Americans. Under Modi, there is new-found respect for Brand India," Naik states.

> The Indian government has realized the value
> of creating world class roads, highways, and
> railways to move people and goods across the
> country, to reduce poverty.

The Union Budget for the fiscal year 2023-24, announced by Finance Minister Sitharaman, raised the capital expenditure on infrastructure for the first time to an all-time high of ₹10 trillion. This is 33 per cent more than the previous year, and 3.3 per cent of India's gross domestic product. The Indian government has realized the value of creating world class roads, highways, and railways to move people and goods across the country, to reduce poverty. Modi's vision was hailed by Corporate India. Naik says that L&T is well poised to cash in on the opportunities—it will be one of the leading beneficiaries of the government's ₹10 trillion capital expenditure. As of March 31, 2024, revenues clocked in at ₹2,21,113 crore, while Profit After Tax reached ₹13,059 crore, registering a 21% and 25% growth respectively.

There are many things that set L&T apart from other players, and Naik is quick to point them out. "You show me one company in the world which is like L&T. In consumer goods there are ten companies, in oil and petrochemicals there are five of six companies, in the auto sector and similar segments there are several. But L&T is unique as we have a presence in several sectors. We are engaged in the upper end of the technology spectrum, manufacturing nuclear reactors, nuclear submarines, equipment and systems for refining and process industry, aerospace missions to the moon and Mars, and howitzers (K9 Vajra).... And what keeps us engaged at the end of the day is that we are doing something which directly helps the nation."

And that more or less conforms to Naik's youthful ambition of working for a company that is engaged in nation-building. With a trace of justifiable pride, he says, "I have led the rebuilding of L&T—65% from scratch—and the rest through total transformation. I feel very happy and grateful that I have had the opportunity to be of service to the company which is my life."

THE FUTURE WITH SNS

SN Subrahmanyan, the new chairman of Larsen & Toubro from October 2023, prefers to keep a low profile. In an interview at L&T's old headquarters in Ballard Estate, he says that he is a "boring CEO of a boring company." But don't let his self-deprecation fool you.

SNS, as he is widely known in the corporate world, has a calm exterior but is a tough taskmaster when it comes to the execution of projects. He was chosen by Naik personally to be his successor as CEO in 2017. SNS's office in Andheri, Mumbai, has a large television set which shows live footage from all the project sites across India. The idea is to keep a hawk eye on all the large projects, so that these projects are completed in time and there is no cost overrun.

Any delay costs the company its brand image, apart from financial costs. Take for example the prestigious Mumbai Metro Line 3 project, connecting Aarey Colony in North Mumbai to Cuffe Parade in South Mumbai. Two segments of this project bagged by L&T were completed on time and handed over to the State government. The rest of the project—comprising five of the seven segments of line 3— was constructed by other companies who didn't complete in time, thus delaying the entire Metro corridor.

SNS, a soft-spoken and affable man who operates from L&T's old British-era building in Ballard Estate in South Mumbai, credits Naik for the transformation of L&T into a global giant. He says that L&T now operates in three broad areas: engineering, procurement, and construction (EPC) of large projects; software services like those of LTIMindtree and L&T Technology Services; and L&T Finance Holdings. SNS was earlier leading the construction business from Chennai, and was handpicked by Naik to spearhead L&T into the next phase of its journey.

"In the last 5-6 years since I took over, we have tried to bring enormous focus into these businesses. After I moved out of construction, we found it difficult to get one leader for the entire construction business, which was a big business segment for us. Hence, we broke the construction business into four broad parts with a leader in each vertical," says SNS. The verticals had contributed to the growth in revenue from ₹14,000 crore in 2011 to ₹1 trillion by 2024.

Similarly, in the energy space, SNS brought in a leader and gave additional charge of green energy for better coordination. Under hydrocarbons, the company was broken up into onshore and offshore businesses, to create more leadership positions in the company. "We have now started looking out for business opportunities not only in India, but also in the Middle East, with special emphasis on client relationships and doing projects on time with quality and safety. This brought in the desired results, and there is a huge order backlog of nearly ₹4.5 trillion to ₹4.7 trillion with the company," SNS says.

At any given time, L&T has at least 10 to 12 mega projects with a value of $700 million (₹5,800 crore) and over going on, thus increasing the pressure on the management. "It is not easy for any organization to simultaneously work on such a high number of mega projects, as this requires a huge leadership at all levels including at the project level, at the business level, at procurement level, and at accounts and administration levels. This means a lot of talent has to be mobilized, and that is helping this pace of growth that is showing in L&T," SNS elaborates.

L&T places an enormous emphasis on client relationships, timely delivery of projects, and most importantly, safety and quality—which has turned out to be its secret sauce of success. Under SNS, high priority has been placed especially on project management leadership, client relationships, and tackling situations on the ground. The project has to first be bagged from the government or companies by participating in the auctions, and then, completed on time.

SNS observes, "Due to this emphasis on project delivery and quality, we are seeing positive results across the organization. In manufacturing, we went through the business in detail. We found out that certain verticals are not making money so we had to remove them. We reimagined our factories to become Factory 4.0. At the shop floor now, one welder is doing four jobs, and four different wellheads are doing welding, which is very unique... few companies have attempted that."

The company also introduced robots at the factory floors to expedite completion of orders, and at the same time, create a safer work environment for its employees. Some of the company's next gen factories—like the defence factory in Coimbatore—make missiles, and are now heavily robotized. Even at the heavy engineering workshop at Hazira, robots are taking over the key functions to complete the orders for Indian and overseas clients in time.

The company has also taken help of sensorization—a modern technology trend to insert many similar sensors in any device—which helps in quality improvement. Most of the products go out exactly on time or even before time—a huge achievement for the L&T workshop. "These initiatives have brought in a reputation that we can do any complex project in Hazira for the entire world, and very few companies in the world can do it," says SNS.

A major challenge faced by the company was during the Covid-19 pandemic, when the world shut down in March 2020 to prevent the spread of the disease. But despite the challenges and limitations brought about by the pandemic, many of L&T's products were delivered on time.

"This was stunning even for us, because the workmen were not attending workshops and the staff was not there. But people struggled and managed to see that our obligations are kept up. This has given its own reputation and enhanced the quality of the brand, and the way people look at us," SNS says. All these measures taken in the last few years have made a big difference in the production workflow, which has several benefits for the conglomerate.

As L&T's shops are now working at full steam after the 2020 pandemic and lockdowns, SNS is preparing the companies to face new challenges.

In the infotech vertical, the merger of L&T Infotech and Mindtree was completed to get synergistic benefits. "In my opinion, the leadership therein did a fantastic job of putting both the companies together. The first priority was to revive Mindtree's profitability, which was hardly 8 per cent. The new management brought it up to 14-15 per cent. The companies also developed a good relationship with the clients. Earlier, LTI was more an ERP (enterprise resource planning) platform and Mindtree was more of a user experience, customer experience kind of company. We brought the strengths of both companies together," SNS explains.

One of the first tasks for SNS in the LTI and Mindtree merger was to select a leader for the merged entity. Debashish Chatterjee, hired from rival Cognizant, was tasked to lead the merged entity from November 2022. The process of getting permissions from the statutory authorities towards the merger was managed in a very cordial manner; both teams were merged in a positive environment. "Enormous time was spent on identifying systems, choosing systems, which software is better. Both companies have come up with their own ways and therefore each one has its own working style," SNS says while recalling the early days of the merger.

To emerge as a global company, the world's best system was procured for work process, procurement approvals, work order approvals, and process approvals, and was finally put together by the management. "This was done in a very open and democratic way. We conducted a lot of workshops and the leadership teams were brought together and as a result, we did not experience much attrition," SNS recounts. "Today we are seeing the benefits because, in spite of all these headwinds, etc., we are continuing to grow both companies in the IT space. The succession was managed in such a way that there was no upheaval."

In L&T Technology Services, a listed entity, the senior leader Dr. Keshab Panda retired, and Amit Chadha took over as the CEO in April 2021. It was again a very smooth exercise that did not cause any upheaval in the ranks. Under the new leadership, both companies (LTIMindtree and LTTS) are continuing to grow, demonstrating the smooth transition under SNS.

SNS recalls Naik's greatest contributions, including the creation of the employee trust that owns 14 per cent of the company's stock. "Thanks to the employee trust, the company has become more secure. The takeover threat from corporate raiders was removed... Though people like me were not exposed to the trust—as we were way down the hierarchy to understand what was happening—we later understood the unique scheme created by Naik," SNS observes.

SNS says that before the trust owned a substantial chunk of shares, not many people in the company spoke of creating shareholder value. "I think this concept of creating shareholder value was driven very hard by Naik, and it was very clear within the company right from the days I used to know him... (Now) most of our meetings end up with talking about what is the profitability, what is the price-to-earnings multiples, what is the shareholder value, etc. For people like me, though we had done management, etc., it had still not gone into the head that ultimately this company is owned by the shareholders, and we have to create value for shareholders," SNS says.

> The principle Naik instilled was that the company should make high enough profits and drive up the multiples, and thus the share value—making it resistant to raiders.

The principle Naik instilled was that the company should make high enough profits and drive up the multiples, and thus the share value—making it resistant to raiders. "I think that is very relevant and clearly captured by us... that made a lot of difference to how we view ourselves." SNS mentions that before Naik became CEO, the company was mostly focused on the completion of projects. "Now we make things that make India proud, and of course, make our shareholders proud. The contribution of Naik in thwarting takeover threats, creating employee trust, and then driving new businesses with a lot of passion and emotion made a big difference to L&T and its people."

SNS recounts that the template to create new businesses was started by Naik, who saw an opportunity in several previously unexplored sectors for L&T. The technology companies were started by Naik in the 1990s when Infosys, TCS, and Wipro had already made big inroads in the industry. By September 2023, both LTIMindtree and LTTS were worth about ₹2 trillion in market valuation. Naik was also instrumental in setting up the financial services business as a separate unit, which now has a market capitalization of about ₹35,000 crore (end-2023). The total market valuation of L&T Group, with its listed IT and finance subsidiaries, is about ₹6 trillion as of September 2023.

As SNS says, "This value has been created by Naik and we have to thank him for this achievement... Also the way Naik brought about many changes in human relations was exceptional. He introduced the management development program, sent people abroad for the executive development program, and introduced the rating system."

Naik changed L&T completely since he took over, and that's the platform the next generation has today. "From 2016-17, when Naik had taken a back seat and allowed me to play a larger role in the running of the company, I think my emphasis has been to look at it from that point of view and then take it forward," SNS elaborates.

"The early days with my mentor, A Ramakrishna, and later in my career with KV Rangaswamy helped me to reach where I am today. Later, Naik spotted me... and provided me with the freedom to do things in my way. And when we are provided with that kind of freedom and we have the best team who can achieve the company's goals, I think the company has developed into what it is today," he says.

SNS now leads the company on the template set by Naik. "My mentors have played an enormous part in shaping what I am today," he says. It was not an easy journey for him, as he had a construction background. The company was started as a manufacturing company, and none of the heads from the construction vertical were inducted into the corner room before him. "Therefore, I think Naik has taken an enormous effort to also settle me in this position, and to convince the board and shareholders that I'm... the right person to succeed him."

> Since L&T is not a family-run company, the leaders must gain the trust of all colleagues, because a team runs these enormous businesses, and their colleagues are also great achievers by themselves.

Since L&T is not a family-run company, the leaders must gain the trust of all colleagues, because a team runs these enormous businesses, and their colleagues are also great achievers by themselves. "It's not that only I have completed large projects; the other leaders have also done huge projects, and some of them have even done large projects outside the company, and therefore one has to earn their respect," SNS reiterates. His main job is to make other leaders also comfortable. "The transition from Naik has been managed very well... we would like to see how to take it forward in an amicable manner."

The goal now is to expand into newer markets. L&T has been synonymous with India's growth story—its growth between 2014 and 2023 has been phenomenal. Under Naik and SNS, the company focused on landing orders from overseas markets; these countries now recognize the quality of work done by L&T. By end-2023, almost one-fourth of L&T's orders of its total of ₹4.12 trillion is expected to be from the overseas markets.

L&T is positive about the future due to the economic stability and strong leadership in India, prudent fiscal management, and several initiatives taken by the Modi government, including free trade agreements being signed with several governments. "The emphasis on *atmanirbharta*, the introduction of the GST, the RERA (Real Estate (Regulation and Development) Act) 2016 has created an atmosphere where the understanding of the rules is easier and red tape has reduced," SNS adds. "There is a vibrant atmosphere now where companies like us find it a lot easier to do business in India. India is very important from that point of view and we hope these policies will continue."

L&T's growth will be fuelled by the India-Middle East-Europe Economic Corridor (IMEC) that would create opportunities for Indian companies. IMEC is an Indian government-led project that aims at transporting goods from Indian ports to Fujairah in the UAE by ship and then by train to Haifa Port in Israel. The containers will then move to Europe, with several countries joining the alliance. This project was undertaken to compete with China's Belt and Road Initiative, which ships Chinese exports across the world via roads and ports built by Chinese companies.

Another priority for L&T is to create more employment opportunities in the country, even as it already employs around three lakh people in India. "We would like to grow employment in the country and construction is one area where we can create a lot of employment. So our growth is important from that point of view," SNS notes.

The company is also looking at the Middle East markets to grow its businesses in the future, with mega orders coming from the region, including from Algeria. The growth is attributed mainly to energy transition, rising oil prices, the Russia-Ukraine war, and other geopolitical factors which are contributing to increased construction activity in the region. Per SNS, as oil prices remain volatile, these countries are looking to develop their economies by encouraging other industries, including services. Saudi Arabia is on a very positive path, and in the process of rolling out deep-rooted economic reforms. The country is leading in energy transition, including to alternative energy sources such as solar, wind, and hydrogen.

All these changes are resulting in massive orders for L&T from Saudi Arabia. The backlog hit $17 billion, which is almost 30 per cent of L&T's orders—thanks to the relationship with most of their top companies, including Aramco, SABIC, Arabian Construction Company, and Ma'aden. "We have looked at other opportunities in the region but at the moment, the idea is to stay focused and not get into too much of experimentation. Diversification is going to be rare and thin with me, and we will continue to focus on what we do... there's enormous things to do within the areas that we are in," comments SNS on L&T's priorities in the years to come.

"Some related diversifications would be required, but not too much and therefore that's the way it's going to be. So in a way, it's going to be boring leadership with a boring company."

∞

Twenty five metres below Mumbai in a metro tunnel, L&T's engineers are busy giving final touches to the

Nariman Point metro station. Once complete, the swanky project would connect South Mumbai to the airport directly and give a fillip to the city's creaky infrastructure. L&T's engineers say they have completed the tunnelling and station construction work before the deadline, and will hand over the project to the state government.

"The topography of Mumbai is not easy. Due to sea water seepage, we had to build additional concrete walls on the sea side before tunnel boring machines could start their work. The CEO would call almost daily to ask about the progress and whether we are facing any issues. We are happy to report that we are ahead of schedule," says L&T's project engineer Palvinder Singh, while proudly showing the work done by the company.

"As L&T, we can't let the country down."

CITATIONS

IIMA. "Shri A M Naik." *IIMA*, Indian Institute of Management Ahmedabad, 2023, www.iima.ac.in/node/1047

Naik, A.M. "Chairman's Speech Delivered at the 78th Annual General Meeting of L&T" [Speech transcript], August 9, 2023, archives.nseindia.com/corporate/LT_090 82023151220_IntimationAGMSpeech.pdf

4.

RAYMOND

The Post-pandemic Success Story

When Gautam Hari Singhania, 59-year-old chairman and managing director of India's most well-known fabric brand—Raymond— took over the company from his father, celebrated aviator Vijaypat Singhania, in 2000 as Chairman, the group was a diversified conglomerate with disparate businesses from steel and cement, to male contraceptives, and even shaving cream. Set up in 1925 as a wool mill at Thane near India's financial capital of Mumbai, Raymond initially supplied blankets to the British armed forces in the country. Its name originated from two British directors at the mill— Albert Raymond and Abraham Jacob Raymond.

In 1944, Lala Kailashpat Singhania purchased Raymond from its British owners, before India gained independence from Britain in 1947. The mill was then producing coarse woollen blankets and small quantities of low-cost woollen garments. Since then, Raymond began a steady process of adopting new technological advancements, which led to its manufacturing superior quality fabrics. Now, the company has 19 factories in the country, and one in the East African nation of Ethiopia.

> Raymond's retail journey started in 1958 when
> its first showroom opened in King's Corner at
> Ballard Estate in Mumbai.

Raymond's retail journey started in 1958 when its first showroom opened in King's Corner at Ballard Estate in Mumbai. The showroom helped the company's management seek feedback directly from its customers. By 1980, Vijaypat Singhania—the son of Lala Kailashpat Singhania—was handed the reins as chairman of Raymond. He is an AMP Alumnus from Harvard and a highflyer in spirit and deed, receiving the Tenzing Norgay National Adventure Award, as well as a Padma Bhushan. During his tenure, the Raymond group forayed into several new areas such as polyester filament yarn, indigo denim, cold-rolled steel, prophylactics, and air charter services.

Today, the company employs over 30,000 people; beyond its own retail network, Raymond supplies readymade clothes to overseas companies including U.S. department store operator JCPenney. In India, the company competes with multinational fashion retail chains such as Marks & Spencer and Zara, along with local fabric makers like Bombay Dyeing and Grasim Industries. Since its inception, Raymond has expanded way beyond its core business, and now runs a successful real estate division which builds and sells apartments on the outskirts of Mumbai.

Over the last century, Raymond has survived uncertain times including the war of independence, the stifling 'licence raj' till the late eighties, the economic liberalization of the early nineties, 2016's demonetization, and the Goods and Services Tax (GST) of the Modi era, apart from devastating global events including World War II and technological disruption.

But the most critical event in Raymond's history was the Covid-19 pandemic that dried up its cash flows and almost shut down the company. It was the Singhania-led team that made sure the company not only survived the pandemic, but returned to profitability.

"Despite several disruptions like the Ukraine war, rising interest rates overseas, and talks of recession in the West, our export order book is full," Gautam Singhania told Dev Chatterjee in an interview at Raymond's headquarters in a plush building in southern Mumbai that houses one of the company's offices and his personal residence. The area is home to several billionaires like Mukesh Ambani and Kumar Mangalam Birla, with the property fetching some of the highest prices in the world.

"Our real estate sales are up three times after Covid, when compared to the same period of 2019 before Covid, and we expect this trend to continue," says Singhania, a renowned auto enthusiast, who set up the Super Car Club of India to restore and maintain antique vehicles. He asserts that India can compete with other key garment-producing nations such as Vietnam and Bangladesh, as it offers everything from cotton cultivation to ginning and stitching. "There is a huge potential for India," he notes.

TAKING ON THE COMPETITION

The winds of change in Raymond were initiated with the opening up of the Indian economy in 1991 by the then Narasimha Rao government.

The winds of change in Raymond were initiated with the opening up of the Indian economy in 1991 by the then Narasimha Rao government. As in the rest of India Inc. prior to liberalization, competition from foreign brands was almost nil for Raymond and other local conglomerates. Singhania, who was already on the Raymond board at this time, realized that the company would have to change its strategy by playing to its strengths.

"At the time of liberalization of the economy in 1991, our biggest strength was the large distribution network in the country. We were already a big brand in India, and we thought of creating our own brands rather than depending on international licences and bringing those international brands into our world," recalls SL Pokharna, President of

Raymond Group, at Raymond's silken boardroom in the multi-storeyed headquarters facing the Arabian Sea.

"We invested heavily in our brands as we realized that sooner or later, competition from the international brands will come. Hence, before their entry, we wanted to deeply penetrate the market so that everyone talked about the Raymond brand only. Even if a foreign brand comes to India, they would need a local partner for distribution. We planned to capture the markets from large cities to tier 3 and tier 4 towns; now we have a network of stores all the way to district level towns," says Pokharna.

The company also focused on customer centricity to gain customer loyalty and adapt to market changes effectively. "We created trust in the minds of customers that the quality of our product would be so high that customers may get tired of wearing Raymond suits but the product will not fail; that's the strength of our quality. Since the beginning, excellence and quality of the products was the main motto of the group," Pokharna notes. The quality culture was built over the last few decades, with the company deciding to export products to Europe and the United States, while business thrived in India.

Pokharna explains how product quality is ensured in Raymond. Most people would not be able to detect minute defects in fabric; specially appointed quality assurance coordinators, also known as 'production-in-charge', spot these modest defects in order to preserve the fineness of products and the interest of customers. "The production-in-charge puts down the fabric on the inspection table, calls the team, and with the help of a marker, highlights the defects. The assistant manager, one of the first lines of managers, will decide that the product will not go to the market, and the defective product will be sold as "seconds". In Raymond, the manager is authorized to reject products as long as 10,000 metres if he detects a defective fabric. The quality of the product is monitored very minutely," he explains.

In the company's review meetings, the quality of the product is the first point of discussion on their agenda. Any complaints on the quality front are discussed threadbare. "Let's say we have received 5 per cent complaints on our products sold—we aim to reduce it to 3 per cent. We would like to know whether the quality complaints have been reduced in the production side or in the market side. We don't want a scenario when production staff is pushing the material into the market," Pokharna says.

The entire organization including the production, marketing, and others are finely tuned to produce quality products. Pokharna divides Raymond's journey into four eras: the first quadrant is the pre-independence era, the second the post-independence era, the third the pre-liberalization era and, finally, the post-liberalization era from 1991. He maintains that in the eyes of customers, the company's brand stood at number one through all these eras. "Something has been done right, and very well. Delegation has been made to the production and marketing department, with zero interference from the management. The idea was not to suppress any complaints on quality," he says.

After the Indian market opened up, several Chinese products arrived with pseudo-international brand names. The Chinese products were priced far lower than Raymond, but customers soon realized the vast difference in quality.

After the Indian market opened up, several Chinese products arrived with pseudo-international brand names. The Chinese products were priced far lower than Raymond, but customers soon realized the vast difference in quality. "The Indian customer wanted to buy a product from a place which is very authentic, and if the product does not perform, they can throw the product back to the shop. So we provided that opportunity to the customer," Pokharna explains about the quality of Raymond products.

"A customer can compare our brand with any brand globally, and performance-wise, we will be the best. If the product does not perform, they can come back and return it to the shop and we replace everything," says Pokharna, Man Friday to Singhania.

To make sure that the quality of their product remains premium, the company has also built its own army of tailors, giving them world class training. "We faced a shortage of tailors as the younger generation was not interested in getting into the profession, even though it is a very profitable business," he notes. Tailoring services became an additional source of income for the franchises— the revenue generated by each franchise from this service is shared between the franchise owners and the tailors.

It's a win-win deal for all stakeholders. While Raymond franchises sell fabric, they have managed to keep the tradition of tailoring alive, training and supporting tailors in their trade. "The franchises realized that providing tailoring services is a great opportunity for an additional income stream, as they made money earlier only on selling the fabric. The company did a survey of tailors and found that they worked in very dingy and congested environments. Sometimes, the master tailor would not pass on their knowledge to the next generation. So, the company decided to develop tailoring skills, by setting up tailoring excellence centres across the country for capacity building among the tailors," the president says.

Soon after liberalization, Indian companies started divesting businesses which were unrelated to their

Soon after liberalization, Indian companies started divesting businesses which were unrelated to their core business.

core business. As the market leader in the textile and engineering businesses, Raymond eventually decided to sell its cement and steel businesses. "We had a plant in Nasik to make steel and it was sold to ThyssenKrupp of Germany in 1998. Similarly, Raymond Synthetic was sold to Reliance Industries, and the cement unit business was sold to LafargeHolcim. We decided to bring the focus back to the two verticals of textiles and engineering, to remain in the top three companies in the segment," Pokharna recounts. "We didn't want to be a small fish in a large pond."

"Being the fifth, sixth or the tenth player in any market does not give us scale, or premium quality; it does not enable us to reach and make a decent mark in the country, so we had to sell those businesses which were laggards," he observes. Pokharna says this was also the reason why, in 2023, Raymond sold its consumer products businesses too. "We sold the FMCG business to such a partner (Godrej) who has the ability to take the journey forward to the next level."

Due to its placement in the market, Raymond is at the pinnacle; it has evolved into an aspirational brand, supported by the customers' discretionary spending. Investing in Raymond fabric is considered an indulgence, one that elevates the customers' social standing—much like driving a Benz or sporting a Rolex watch. "Raymond as a brand has big strengths with a legacy of 100 years... We have seen several ups and downs in the country and we continue to remain at the top, and our core strengths remain the same. Today, in terms of reach, we are present in 600 plus cities in India, and growing."

> Investing in Raymond fabric is considered an indulgence, one that elevates the customers' social standing—much like driving a Benz or sporting a Rolex watch.

The company was cruising comfortably until the Covid-19 pandemic hit the world.

LEARNING FROM THE PANDEMIC

The Covid pandemic, which shut down almost all of Raymond's 1,400 clothing showrooms, was an eye-opener; Singhania knew that the company had to either perform or perish. Over the last few decades, the BSE listed group has shed several businesses so that it remained relevant in the ever-changing business landscape. But the company was clearly not ready for a disruption like the one spawned by the Covid-19 pandemic.

It was not only Raymond. The pandemic was a crippling blow for the entire Indian retail sector. Several retail chains like the Future Group—once the barometer of Indian consumer spending—shut down completely, and were sent to bankruptcy court by its lenders to sell assets. Others had to restructure their debt or scale down their operations, laying off thousands of employees.

During the pandemic, Singhania strengthened the senior leadership team throughout various management tiers. The group hired Amit Agarwal of the JSW group as Chief Financial Officer to slash costs and reduce debt—to improve overall financial prudence, with a mandate of restructuring the group's finances. Singhania's Team A included longtime family loyalist SL Pokharna, who was looking after commerce and logistics for the group as its president.

The lockdown announced by the government in March 2020 impacted Raymond as it shut down stores and factories across the country, while employees worked from home. Pokharna says, "The shutdown was actually a blessing in disguise for us. Before the pandemic, we had accumulated a lot of fat like the human body; we were ignoring taking any steps until a doctor steps in to put us on drugs. When the pandemic hit us, sales collapsed and we were in a big logjam."

Pokharna and Agarwal had to revisit each and every cost to prevent the undoing of the company. A 'Distress Cabinet' was formed to assess the situation and take decisions. "We scanned through every single item of cost. The question we asked was, *'Is this cost is really required?'* If we ask the same question to the department heads, then their obvious answer would be yes. But we took a hard look and cut costs by ₹900 crore in the first year of Covid," Pokharna said.

"We would spend days debating whether and how we can run this business without having that particular cost item. A classic example of cutting costs was to reduce trade expenditure. Before Covid, we would call dealers from all across the country to showcase our new collections, and pay for 4,000 people's stay and food for a week in Mumbai," Pokharna recalls. The company would end up spending ₹50-60 crores each year in the dealers' conference, labelling it a booking expenditure.

The dealers would make their advance bookings so that they were able to receive the products and sell them in their stores. Pokharna explains, "We have a massive booking hall in Thane of around 50,000 square feet. The dealers would come from across India and book their products for the summer or winter season. Starting 2020, we moved the entire event digitally... thus saving on costs."

The company also took a hard look at its apparel business— which had revenues of ₹1,500 crore per annum at the time of the pandemic. "The sales were ₹1,500 crore, but we had built an organization with a cost structure of a company with sales of ₹5,000 crore. This had no ability to sustain, so we had to cut a lot of costs there. We also had advertising spends for various sub-brands, but we decided to advertise only Raymond as the mother brand, and axed the rest," Pokharna says.

This made the fundamental difference in its turnaround strategy. According to Pokharna, "We looked at every single cost and cut the flab in the organization. With this, of the ₹2,500 crore of costs, we managed to shave off ₹400 crore and made sure that this cost never comes back." The company also shut down non-profit-making stores, and renegotiated rental contracts which were very high during the pre-Covid era.

> The company also shut down non-profit-making stores, and renegotiated rental contracts which were very high during the pre-Covid era.

In his communication to his shareholders, Singhania—who owns half of the company's shares—recalled how the first quarter (April to June 2020) was the "darkest hour" for the company, when neither real estate nor textile businesses had any idea about how to deal with the pandemic, or were even aware of the severity of its impact. "Given the lack of short-term visibility, it was the time to introspect and undertake immediate measures to stay on course. The global pandemic has presented such a crisis, and that too on a scale many of us have never experienced or could have predicted," Singhania wrote.

The pandemic, per Singhania, necessitated the company to look at the dual fundamental metrics of any business: liquidity and costs. "The first two quarters of the fiscal were committed to ensure that these metrics are prioritized... We looked at all the costs that could be curtailed through cost rationalization, thereby conserving the cash. We reworked on all operational efficiencies, resulting in reduced working capital that helped in paring the debt during the financial year," he explained in his message.

The pandemic, per Singhania, necessitated the company to look at the dual fundamental metrics of any business: liquidity and costs.

As the retail network slowly opened in the last two quarters of fiscal 2021, the company witnessed pent-up demand coupled with festivities, and a high number of wedding dates. "The consumer sentiments improved during the year, with the fourth quarter witnessing top-line growth that was driven by branded textiles; and we closed the fiscal with a profitable fourth quarter," Singhania said. "We took some tough decisions during the year that reaped results for us as we cut debt in FY 2020-21, demonstrating our resilience, especially during the pandemic."

During pandemic lockdowns, the company faced multiple challenges with rising costs and stagnating sales. "At that time, we were not the most competitive players across all businesses. We had such a great reputation about the brand and the product quality... primarily in the suiting business, but not in all businesses. Another problem faced by the company was the drying up of working capital as several dealers stopped payment to the company. Some dealers delayed payments for over 180 days, and were still asking for more time," Pokharna remembers.

By October 2021, the situation had improved with customers coming back to the stores, and the company decided to tighten the screws on accountability. When dealers from their franchise network sought more material, the company put its foot down. "We made it clear that if the dealer is not paying dues of over 120 days, then we are not supplying products. In the month of October 2021, we were sitting with high inventory, and we were worried about the sales. By the end of the month, our suiting fabric sales picked up gradually, and we managed to touch our monthly target of ₹200 crore of sales, and lost only ₹7-8 crores of sales as the rest of the dealers paid," Pokharna narrates.

As the next step, dealers were asked to pay their dues within 90 days and then, in 60 days by December. The working capital cycle, which had stretched to an average of 110 days, slowly reduced to 55 days—which helped the company improve its cash flows. The restructuring of the company during the pandemic era not only ensured efficiency, but also led to cost optimization measures related to sales and marketing, reduction in manpower, rentals, and other costs.

DEVELOPING FINANCIAL DISCIPLINE

The Covid-hit FY 2020-21 witnessed a major change in the consolidated debt structure of Raymond; short-term debt to long-term debt as a percentage improved from 79:21 in March 2020 (pre-Covid year) to 17:83 in March 2021, with long-term debt having 3-10 year maturities. Nonessential capital expenditure was also deferred to maintain liquidity.

The consolidated revenue for the year dropped to ₹3,648 crores, as the pandemic significantly affected revenues, especially in the first six months of the financial year. In the second half, the rebound in the market with gradual recovery of consumer sentiments led to a bounce back in sales to almost three times in the second half of the year, as compared to the first six months of the year.

In fact, in the fourth quarter, Raymond's consolidated revenues grew by 9 per cent over the previous year, against the backdrop of strong recovery in demand. Its continued focus on cost rationalization measures brought in efficiencies which led to its operating costs being considerably reduced by 40 per cent as compared to the previous year—from ₹2,207 crores in FY 2020 to just ₹1,320 crores in FY 2021.

"During the pandemic, we were sitting on 90 per cent of our debt as short-term debt which was falling due in 30 days, and 45 days. So a debt of ₹10 crores, ₹50 crores or ₹100 crore was maturing every second day. But at the same time there was zero sales due to the pandemic, and the collection from the retail stores were not coming. We were in almost a hand-to-mouth situation, and we were not sure whether we would be able to pay salaries or pay vendors," relates Amit Agarwal, Group CFO of Raymond, in an interview in mid-2023, about the harrowing Covid days.

Raymond, therefore, had to take a very aggressive approach to reduce its debt—by asking its banks for help. "We managed to refinance our debt book from short-term to long-term debt of over next 4-5 months. By January 2021, we had converted the entire book to a three-year loan and the repayment pressure was eased," says Agarwal.

"We were able to maintain liquidity in the range of ₹550 crores to ₹650 crores of cash and cash equivalents throughout the year. Over recent times, the company has embarked on a deleveraging plan, and has undertaken multiple steps in that direction with the purpose of enhancing shareholder value," Agarwal wrote in the company's annual report in 2021.

Just before the pandemic, the company had infused ₹350 crores in December 2019 as a preferential issue from net proceeds from sale of land by an associate company, and utilized the entire amount to cut debt.

Just before the pandemic, the company had infused ₹350 crores in December 2019 as a preferential issue from net proceeds from sale of land by an associate company, and utilized the entire amount to cut debt. The deleveraging strategy in the six consecutive quarters improved its net debt equity ratio steadily, and stood at 0.65 times as of March 2021, as compared to 0.75 times in March 2020.

Even as the company raised long-term debt from banks and repaid its short-term debt, it placed more of an emphasis on collections and reduction of inventory. This measure helped the company to reduce its net working capital by ₹738 crores from ₹1,855 crores in March 2020 to ₹1,117 crores by March 2021.

The improvement in sales recovery along with efforts in controlling operational expenditures and working capital management resulted in generating operating cash flow of ₹702 crores, and free cash flows of ₹417 crores during the year. This cash flow was utilized for reducing consolidated net debt level by ₹443 crores by March 2021.

All these factors led to a 21 per cent reduction in net working capital (NWC) over 3 years until March 2023, bringing it down to 69 NWC days. 'Net working capital' refers to the difference between a company's current assets and liabilities. The NWC is a measure of a company's liquidity, and its ability to meet short-term obligations and fund operations. The company also rationalized its stock keeping units (SKUs) in an effort to reduce its inventories and release cash flow.

GATHERING THE COMMUNITY

Pokharna sums up the situation in the Covid years, "We identified that there were a lot of issues in the apparel business. One, we were stuck with huge inventory across multiple points within our warehouses. Second, we had a completely demotivated team of employees who were uncertain about their future, and the third problem was how to retain our market as the competition was spreading rumours that Raymond apparel was in trouble."

About 200 non-profitable stores of the company's brands were closed during Covid.

About 200 non-profitable stores of the company's brands were closed during Covid. For the remaining stores, the management decided to renegotiate the rentals with landlords and reduce rents by up to 50 per cent. Some of the company stores were also offered as franchises on a revenue sharing model. Pokharna explains that these systems were put in place to contain predictable losses.

Singhania's Distress Cabinet to bring the company back on track had only three members—Pokharna, Agarwal, and Narayan. "Beyond this, I made it clear that I will not take any interference from anybody till we put the business back on the rails. After this was agreed, we started the journey, and I had a meeting with all the vendors. I travelled across the country and talked to them over Zoom calls. Because of my old association with the dealers, I enjoyed reasonably good credibility and trust," Pokharna says about the Covid fight back.

The dealers were open to cooperating with the company, since they had great trust in the septuagenarian Pokharna. He now asked the marketing team to start a campaign by putting large hoardings across the country in several key junctions—the message was being sent out to the competition that Raymond was back in business. The marketing campaign gave further confidence to the traders and dealers, since the company was willing to invest in the brand. At the same time, a social media campaign was launched to target the younger generation, which too boosted confidence in the market.

"We had a vendors meeting to apprise them of the situation—that we have started production in full swing. We also took help from two stalwarts and our partners for decades—Suryakant Jaipuria from New Delhi and Gautam Jain from Hyderabad. Both are strong Raymond supporters, and their businesses grew with Raymond. We told them that the company needs your support to develop confidence among the trade fraternity, as they respect the three of us a lot," Pokharna says. The three old-timers started calling the dealers and traders; the messaging was that Raymond was reviving fast, and would come back strong. In their weekly review meetings, Pokharna, Jain, and Jaipuria would take stock of the situation, and decide on the next course of action to inculcate confidence among the dealers.

At the same time, decision-making was done rapidly with the Distress Cabinet (or 'war room', as Pokharna likes to call it) working in a 24-hour cycle. "The war room had to give its decisions within three hours—even if an issue was raised at 12 AM or 3 AM in the morning. I had authorized my juniors to take decisions, and if they are not able to take the decision then it was escalated to my level. I conveyed to the sales staff that if you want to make any decision which is required to be taken but is not within your authority, then don't hesitate to make it. Later, if I found the decision was right, then I would ratify it immediately, and if the decision was wrong, I would let it pass but with a rider that such decisions should not be taken in the future," Pokharna reminisces.

This immediately bolstered the confidence of the employees, as well as the sentiments of the traders and dealers. "When the employees started feeling that we are empowered to make a decision, then they would work for almost 14-15 hours a day despite travel restrictions. The staff went back to the market with renewed confidence, with large hoardings across the country," says Pokharna, who still prefers calling up people instead of writing emails.

During the post-Covid turnaround, Singhania kept the war room motivated by giving them a free hand at making big picture decisions.

During the post-Covid turnaround, Singhania kept the war room motivated by giving them a free hand at making big picture decisions. "Singhania used to sit in on the review meetings and we used to brief him about the production, sales, and trade meetings. If we disagreed on any issue, we would tell him that this is not the time to do this... We were in June 2021 and we wanted to avoid travel, hence we would hold meetings every Monday without fail, with the top management joining on video calls. We would monitor the production and sales reports closely. Singhania motivated us continuously and his motivation gave us phenomenal strength," Pokharna adds.

Within months of Team A's takeover of the management, the company was EBITDA neutral and by March 2022, Raymond was EBITDA positive.

> The company's retail network is spread across several towns and cities in India and overseas, with stores in nine countries.

Despite shutting down several stores during the pandemic, Raymond has one of the largest retail networks of 1,453 stores including 1,065 retail outlets, 43 made-to-measure, and 345 exclusive brand outlets. It has a dedicated retail space of 2.49 million square feet as of September 2023. The company's retail network is spread across several towns and cities in India and overseas, with stores in nine countries. As part of its asset light strategy, more than 80 per cent of the branded apparel stores are now franchisee-owned, wherein the company incurs minimal capital expenditure to open a store, with land and store space owned by the franchisee, and renovation costs too incurred by the franchisee.

With all the restructuring now behind it, the company plans to expand its retail store network by opening around 200 stores in the next 12-18 months from 2024, mainly through the asset light franchise model.

CASHING IN ON A REAL ESTATE BOOM

The company had a large land bank of 120 acres in the prime location at Thane; it fell back on this vertical to increase its cash flows during the pandemic. The first half of the year was impacted due to lockdowns as there were restrictions on commercial and construction activities. With the lockdown in effect, Raymond, like the remaining real estate companies, engaged with potential buyers through digital and virtual interactive touch-points. This led to sales of 455 units, taking the total inventory sold to 1,387 units till March 2021, with a saleable area of 1.18 million square feet, having a booking value of ₹1,324 crores.

With the phased relaxation of the lockdown, Raymond initiated sales and construction activities, and its realty project gained increasing momentum with around 400 units sold in the second-half of the year. The government's move to reduce stamp duty and lower home loan interest rates also helped it to make sales.

After the pandemic, the demand for housing grew exponentially in India. Customers living in smaller houses had been confined to congested spaces during the pandemic. Of its sales revenue of ₹8,000 crore in FY 2023, the company reported real estate sales of ₹1,100 crore and ₹1,600 crore of booking value.

The company now targets first time homeowners, with gated residential facilities having renowned schools within the complex. The company's strategy is to make land monetization at Thane a critical aspect in unlocking value for Raymond shareholders in the years to come.

Soon after the pandemic, the group started a restructuring of its businesses, with the company's board approving the subsidiarization of Raymond Realty into a wholly-owned subsidiary. A new company called TenX Realty has been incorporated as a step-down subsidiary of Raymond Limited—to increase real estate business for development of land and properties, in line with its plans to expand beyond Thane.

> Soon after the pandemic, the group started a restructuring of its businesses, with the company's board approving the subsidiarization of Raymond Realty into a wholly-owned subsidiary.

EMERGING STRONGER THAN EVER

The resurgent demand for big fat Indian weddings just after the coronavirus pandemic worked out in the company's favour. It was welcome news for Raymond, whose core business remains its dapper suits and fashionable textiles that it churns out for both its own stores and other retailers.

As customers returned to the stores, propelled by a record number of weddings between January and March of 2022, they helped the company report a substantial rise in their average transaction values.

As customers returned to the stores, propelled by a record number of weddings between January and March of 2022, they helped the company report a substantial rise in their average transaction values. The emerging opportunity was tapped by the company to enter the ethnic wear space, wherein it opened stores under the new brand 'Ethnix by Raymond'.

Singhania, who prefers to delegate responsibilities, says a spending spree during the wedding seasons helped Raymond turn the corner. "We have witnessed a sharp turnaround in our sales due to higher consumer spending in our stores following the Covid-19 pandemic," he observes. "With the record wedding season planned in the next few months, I am optimistic that this trend will continue."

The company consolidated its businesses to a consumer business by transferring the apparel business from Raymond Apparel to itself, which brought all major apparel brands including Park Avenue, Colorplus, Parx, and Ethnix by Raymond into the parent.

In the engineering segment, the company's board decided to consolidate the tools & hardware and auto components businesses into JK Files in FY 2022. The consolidation of these businesses that work in a unified fashion under JK Files & Engineering is showcasing exemplary performance, and is likely to derive benefit through synergies.

It was not a surprise, therefore, that by the end of FY 2022, the group recorded its highest-ever EBITDA, and the highest net profit on a consolidated basis in the last 10 years. "Our strategy to focus on the core and recalibrate the fundamental metrics of each business such as revenue, cost, and working capital have reaped rich dividends for the Raymond group. Our focus on cost optimization and significant reduction in our operating costs by ₹453 crores as compared to pre-Covid levels of FY 2020, was critical for our business. The profitability and working capital management have helped in generating free cash flows, thereby reducing our debts drastically," Singhania wrote in his annual communication to the company's shareholders in fiscal 2022.

For the year 2022, the company reported a consolidated revenue of ₹6,348 crores—a strong 74 per cent growth over the pandemic year's revenues of ₹3,648 crores. The firm also reported its highest consolidated EBITDA at ₹881 crores, a margin of 13.9 per cent and net income of ₹260 crores during the year.

Soon after Covid, this facilitated a reduction of net debt by 60 per cent, over the last three to four years. Singhania also undertook a massive restructuring of the group's structure by divesting the consumer products business and announcing the demerger of lifestyle business. A new plan was set in motion to leverage the brand and scale in each category to drive growth. The demerger would unlock value for its shareholders, and also allow investors to invest in either vertical, and not have exposure to a single holding company.

As per plan, in April 2023, Raymond took a major step towards restructuring its businesses when it announced the demerger of the lifestyle business of textile, garment, and shirting into Raymond Consumer Care (RCCL). In its new avatar, Raymond will be a real estate company with investments in engineering and the denim business; RCCL, now a separate entity, would also house the suiting business with manufacturing plants, B2C shirting, and branded apparel with its portfolio of brands.

According to this plan, existing shareholders of Raymond received four shares of RCCL for every five shares held, and post demerger of the lifestyle business, Singhania's stake would be the same at 49.11 per cent in Raymond, whereas his stake would be 54.87 per cent in RCCL, as he infused Rs 1,400 crore into it, enabling a net debt free lifestyle business.

> Raymond took a major step towards restructuring its businesses when it announced the demerger of the lifestyle business of textile, garment, and shirting into Raymond Consumer Care (RCCL).

Raymond also announced its acquisition of 59.25 per cent stake in Maini Precision Products for ₹682 crore, funded by a mix of debt and internal accruals. Ring Plus Aqua, a step-down subsidiary of Raymond, acquired the stake in MPPL funded by own cash of ₹85 crore, debt of ₹342 crore, and internal debt from Raymond of ₹255 crore.

Post-acquisition, Raymond was also consolidating JK Files and Engineering, RPAL and MPPL into a new subsidiary, in which it would hold 66.3 per cent of the new company that will focus on precision engineering products. The plan is to strengthen Raymond's existing engineering business with a complementing business that has presence in the aerospace, electric vehicles, and defence sectors.

Raymond, at the same time, announced the sale of its fast moving consumer goods business housed under RCCL in a slump sale to Godrej Consumer Products for ₹2,825 crore.

The company sold its condom brands KamaSutra and Premium, as well as deodorant brands Park Avenue and KS, to the Godrej group in an all-cash deal in April 2023. The proceeds were utilized to repay its debt of ₹1,029 crore, and the rest was put in liquid investments.

As of September 2023, the Raymond Group turned net debt free and now plans to maintain its net debt free status.

Thanks to the steps taken during and since the pandemic years, the financial risk profile of Raymond is now characterized by healthy capital structure and debt coverage metrics. "The improvement in the operating performance, focused on improving working capital by deploying cash generated during the year, resulted in partial improvement of debt metrics," CARE Ratings noted in December 2023.

The cash in books for both companies also improved from ₹1,411 crore in March 31, 2023, to ₹1,712 crore in September 30, 2023. "The Raymond group has adequate financial flexibility in terms of raising capital from market, and also supported by its owned land bank of around 60 acres excluding around 40 acres currently being developed at a prime location in Thane, which can be developed over the next few years," according to the CARE Ratings report.

Besides, several joint venture projects outside of Thane in Bandra, Mahim, and Sion in Mumbai have revenue potentials of over ₹5,000 crore. Going forward, the company plans to avail debt to fund the real estate projects. However, cash flows from existing real estate projects, and reliance on customer advances for real estate funding are expected to keep debt metrics under control, CARE stated.

Going forward, the company plans to avail debt to fund the real estate projects.

As of fiscal 2023, Indian operations contributed 80 per cent to the company's total revenues and the remainder was from overseas operations. Furthermore, it has a largely integrated presence across the textile value chain right from yarn manufacturing to suiting and shirting fabrics, to garments, denim, apparel, and retailing. "This integrated setup gives Raymond operational flexibility to rationalize costs by managing dependence on outsourced vendors," notes the rating firm.

However, the company is also facing risks in the real estate sector, like inflation due to increases in steel and cement prices. The possibility of any potential price hikes may not be sufficient to offset the entire increase in input cost. Furthermore, CARE warned that current high interest rates and high financing cost for homebuyers may impact the overall demand scenario in the real estate industry.

Raymond, with a market valuation of nearly ₹11,466 crore (as of December 2023) expects to beat its previous sales numbers as consumer spending on new houses and clothes rise substantially. Clothing and textiles continue to account for nearly half the conglomerate's revenues.

Singhania also expects a sharp rise in garment exports as Western retailers look to broaden their supply chains away from China, where strict pandemic lockdowns have overshadowed production. "We reported a sharp rise in sales as our overseas clients ordered more suits and shirts as they sought other suppliers apart from China," he says. Several American and European retail chains are looking for additional suppliers for their stores as part of their China plus one supply chain strategy. As the geo-political relations between China and western countries deteriorated, Indian companies stood to benefit from this development.

In the coming months, Raymond aims to open more stores in smaller towns to cash in on rising consumer spending, while broadening its clothing lines to include more traditional Indian garments—often popular during Hindu wedding rituals. "We have noticed that each customer is now spending higher after the pandemic by as much as 25 per cent to 30 per cent in our stores, when compared to pre-Covid. We are on the cusp of record growth," Singhania predicts.

Pokharna comments that as the company started recovering from the post-pandemic stress, it was time to run, not to walk. The group wanted to cash in on the momentum gained after the restructuring during the pandemic. "The group will have two listed entities, and the plan is to double the market valuation of both entities from the present," Pokharna says. He contends that both real estate and garments will see a massive growth in the years to come, as demand for both products is witnessing growth.

"If you really want to push the envelope, then we think real estate will be the next big thing for us, because there is no limit. For example, when a company is in a commodity business like cement, etc., the growth will be in line with the industry average. But in real estate, we cannot restrict ourselves to Mumbai or Thane, we can expand to other cities," he says.

"In the lifestyle business, we are definitely a national player, and to some extent, an international player. Earlier, Mumbai was the hub of textile companies; now none of the older brands are standing, but we are still in the game apart from Reliance and Arvind. We plan to build the brand in the years to come," Pokharna contends.

"Raymond is here to stay."

CITATION

CARE Ratings Ltd. "Raymond Limited" [Press Release], 28 Dec. 2023, www.careratings.com/upload/CompanyFiles/PR/202312141206_Raymond_Limited.pdf

Raymond Limited. "Strengthening the core", Annual report 2020-21, api.raymond.in/uploads/investor/1658324454873 ANNUAL%20REPORT.pdf

5.

RELIGARE

A Takeover Drama amid Spectacular Turnaround

I n the smog-filled New Delhi winter of 2023, Dr. Rashmi Saluja, the chair of Religare Enterprises—a financial services company—first heard of the Burman family's open offer to acquire the company. The Burman family, owners of the Dabur group, sought to increase their stake by 26 per cent at a cost of ₹2,166 crore, aiming at full control of Religare Enterprises. At the time of the open offer on September 25, 2023, the Burmans already owned 21 per cent of the company.

"The proposed transaction aligns with our vision to create a leading financial services platform encompassing lending, broking, and health insurance services," said Anand Burman, Chairman Emeritus of Dabur India, in a statement. He emphasized that Religare Enterprises was poised for sustained success, and that the Burman family intended to guide the company to become a distinguished financial services platform.

Initially, the Religare board, led by Saluja, responded positively, viewing the acquisition as a step that would strengthen the company's position. However, within days, the board rebelled against the acquisition. "We were taken by surprise by the open offer, as we were not in the loop about the plans," Saluja said in an interview with the author at a tony Mumbai hotel.

Saluja, a doctor by training and former medical advisor to New Delhi's Sir Ganga Ram Hospital, joined the Religare board as an independent director in 2018, and became chairperson by June 2020. Dr. Saluja is credited with leading Religare's board in salvaging the company from bankruptcy, after its former owners were accused of financial fraud.

Dr. Saluja is credited with leading Religare's board in salvaging the company from bankruptcy, after its former owners were accused of financial fraud.

Concerned about the timing of the Burmans' takeover bid, the Religare board immediately contacted Indian regulators, questioning whether the Burmans met the "fit and proper" criteria due to their alleged involvement in financial scams, including those revealed in the Pandora Papers. The board also mentioned that the open offer price of ₹235 per share undervalued the company, and appointed independent appraisers to reassess the shares. The Burman family had previously acquired a 9.9 per cent stake in REL in April 2018, just before Saluja was appointed as an independent director.

The Burman family had previously acquired a 9.9 per cent stake in REL in April 2018, just before Saluja was appointed as an independent director.

Religare Enterprises, established in 1984, owns stakes in a stock broking arm, a health insurance company—Care Health Insurance, and a non-banking lender—Religare Finvest. Care Health Insurance had become the jewel of the group by mid-2023, with peers like Star Health & Allied Insurance valued at over ₹33,500 crore (as of July 2024). Acquiring the parent firm would give the Burmans control of Care Health Insurance, the fastest-rising company in the group in terms of valuation.

$$\sim$$

Fifty-five-year-old Mohit Burman, Chairman of Dabur India, is a well-built man of medium-height with aggressive expansion plans. Under his leadership, the family office made key acquisitions, including Eveready Industries India in 2022. The acquisition of Religare Enterprises was intended to be the Burman family's full-fledged entry into the financial sector, complementing their stakes in Aviva Life Insurance and Universal Sompo General Insurance. The family even owns a stake in the Indian Premier League cricket team Kings XI Punjab.

The rebellion by the Religare board caught the Burmans off guard. "We have no plans to change the existing board of Religare Enterprises after the open offer," Burman said in an interview with the author in Dabur's Fort office in Mumbai. He emphasized the family's intention to invest additional capital in Religare to grow its businesses, citing their longstanding industry presence and compliance with regulatory criteria.

> The open offer by the Burman family to acquire an additional 26 per cent stake would cost them ₹2,116 crore, assuming full acceptance by minority shareholders.

The open offer by the Burman family to acquire an additional 26 per cent stake would cost them ₹2,116 crore, assuming full acceptance by minority shareholders. Religare's shares, which had fallen to as low as ₹17 a share in March 2020, were at ₹271 each in September 2023 when the Burmans made the open offer. The shares soon dropped to ₹223, making the open offer attractive for retail investors.

Burman argued that with the change in promoters, Religare Finvest would become a viable lending entity, and the credit rating of RFL and REL would improve. "We thought this was the right time to make the open offer after five years of being an anchor investor," Burman said, suggesting some people were trying to scuttle the offer for vested interests. The Burmans also raised questions over the grant of Employee Stock Ownership Plans (ESOPs) to Saluja.

InGovern Research Services, a proxy advisory firm, supported the Burmans' arguments, calling for an investigation into Saluja's remuneration and any conflict of interest. They raised concerns about the issuance of ESOPs to Saluja at Care Health Insurance, alleging they were granted at a deep discount, and without proper disclosure to shareholders. InGovern also highlighted discrepancies in the approval process for these ESOPs.

Religare officials countered that the ESOPs were approved by Care Health's board, and the nomination and remuneration committee. They argued that the insurance regulator's guidelines did not require specific approval for the ESOPs granted to Saluja. They emphasized that the ESOPs were for her role as an employee of REL, and not for her non-executive chairperson role at Care Health Insurance.

The Religare board defended Saluja, highlighting her role in the company's resurgence, which saw its market cap grow from under $100 million in March 2018 to about $1 billion by 2023. They refuted the allegations made by InGovern, asserting that the board had worked tirelessly to make Religare a debt-free organization.

The board noted that the Burman family did not inform Saluja of the open offer during an informal meeting with her on September 20, 2023; this informal meet had led to allegations of insider trading when she sold shares shortly thereafter. The board also clarified that the share sale process had been set in motion before the meeting.

As Religare and the Burmans made comments and allegations one after another, tensions escalated and yet another controversy emerged. The Mumbai Police filed a first information report (FIR) against Mohit and Gaurav Burman for their alleged links to a cricket betting syndicate, and the Mahadev betting app. The Burmans, who owned the IPL team Kings XI Punjab, denied the allegations, attributing them to vested interests trying to thwart their acquisition of Religare. The police did not file any charges against the Burmans.

The battle for control of Religare Enterprises had intensified, with both the Burmans and Saluja's board entrenched in their positions.

The battle for control of Religare Enterprises had intensified, with both the Burmans and Saluja's board entrenched in their positions. As the dust slowly settled, the outcome of this corporate struggle remained uncertain for a long time, making it is clear that the stakes were incredibly high for all parties involved.

THE RELIGARE MELTDOWN

To comprehend the revival of Religare and this intense battle over it, one must delve into the company's history. Religare was initially a stock brokerage firm set up in 1982. The Singh brothers, descendants of refugees who fled Pakistan during its bloody partition, managed the company until 2018, when minority shareholders took over. Malvinder and Shivinder Singh amassed a fortune by selling their family jewel, Ranbaxy Pharmaceuticals, to Japan's Daiichi Sankyo in 2008 for $4.8 billion. However, they became entangled in several questionable transactions. While overseeing Religare Enterprises and the Fortis hospital chain, the brothers faced allegations of fund diversion from both companies.

As the finances of Religare Enterprises deteriorated, the company attempted to sell its health insurance subsidiary to the private equity firm True North in April 2017. However, the sale could not be concluded.

In February 2018, Bay Capital, a private equity firm, decided to become a stakeholder and launched an open offer for Religare Enterprises, just a day before the Singh brothers decided to resign from the board. By February 18, 2018, minority shareholders led by Bay Capital, SSG Capital (another private equity firm), and the International Finance Corporation took control of the company; they requested that the market regulator, SEBI, declassify the Singh brothers as promoters.

By June 2018, rating agencies began warning investors that Religare Finvest was haemorrhaging and on the brink of collapse. CARE Ratings downgraded RFL's debt instruments, citing the impact of deteriorating asset quality due to the recognition of a corporate loan book of ₹2,087 crore, and its provisioning of around 50 per cent of the book, resulting in RFL reporting a massive loss of ₹1,103 crore for FY 2018.

The credit ratings agency cautioned that Religare Finvest's bad loans, including the NPAs (Non-Performing Assets) of the corporate loan book, were 141 per cent of the tangible net worth as of end-March 2018. "The ratings also take into account significant de-growth of the loan portfolio during the last 18 months, resulting in an operational net loss during the first half of FY 2018, and qualifying remarks by the auditors regarding their inability to comment on the status and classification on account of adjustment of fixed deposits of ₹750 crore by Lakshmi Vilas Bank (LVB).

If this fixed deposit is not reinstated, it could impact the company's asset quality and capitalization further," CARE Ratings warned. The outlook of the company was negative due to significant pressure on its asset quality, profitability, and capitalization.

> The outlook of the company was negative due to significant pressure on its asset quality, profitability, and capitalization.

The ratings firm reported a slowdown in loan disbursements during FY 2017 and FY 2018, resulting in the company's loan portfolio, excluding off-book assets, declining from ₹12,106 crore on March 31, 2017, to ₹9,797 crore on March 31, 2018, including a corporate loan book of ₹2,407 crore. As RFL's financial health worsened, the Reserve Bank of India mandated adherence to a corrective action plan that prohibited RFL from expanding its credit and investment portfolios, the ratings firm informed investors in June 2018.

> As RFL's financial health worsened, the Reserve Bank of India mandated adherence to a corrective action plan that prohibited RFL from expanding its credit and investment portfolios.

As financials of RFL deteriorated, banks seized pledged shares of the promoters. Malvinder and Shivinder Singh's stake in Religare Enterprises (REL)—the parent entity of RFL—reduced to 3.02 per cent by May 2018. A management change occurred at the REL level, with the Singh brothers stepping down from the board and new members joining, including Siddharth Mehta of Bay Capital; Vikram Talwar, a senior banker with 26 years of experience; and P Vijaya Bhaskar, former Director of the RBI.

To boost its capital, Religare Enterprises planned to raise ₹916 crore in capital, with ₹160 crore from domestic investors like the Burmans, including 25 per cent warrant money of ₹145 crore, and an additional 75 per cent capital from other investors. The remaining ₹83.3 crore of share warrant money from foreign investors required permission from the Ministry of Finance. The management mentioned that the remaining 75 per cent of capital could be called anytime within 18 months of raising the share warrant money. Timely infusion of this capital at the RFL level would be critical for maintaining its capitalization profile.

According to a police complaint cited by the *Indian Express*, RFL allegedly invested ₹750 crore in fixed deposits in Lakshmi Vilas Bank between 2016 and early 2017. In July 2017, RFL claimed it discovered that LVB had credited the proceeds of the deposits to RFL's current account, and debited around ₹724 crore without prior intimation. By December 2017, RFL received a letter stating that some loans were given to RHC Holding and Ranchem Pvt, companies owned by the Singh brothers, using Religare deposits as collateral. RFL claimed LVB did not inform them of placing the fixed deposits as collateral, and subsequently filed a suit against LVB in the Delhi High Court in September, where the matter is pending.

Religare officials stated that the new board and management were making significant efforts to recover as much as possible from its regular, small, and medium-scale businesses and non-core assets to repay over ₹9,000 crore to its lenders. To assist in recovering funds siphoned off through various non-core assets, RFL engaged an expert agency for forensic investigation. This effort aimed to recover misappropriated monies and share them with lenders, which would be a significant step towards the company's revival.

Per the *Indian Express* report, the Singh brothers faced multiple cases, including one filed by Daiichi Sankyo, alleging they siphoned off funds through a complex web of companies from Ranbaxy, sold to the Japanese firm.

Per the *Indian Express* report, the Singh brothers faced multiple cases, including one filed by Daiichi Sankyo, alleging they siphoned off funds through a complex web of companies from Ranbaxy, sold to the Japanese firm. In its

2018 application to the High Court, Daiichi claimed that the Singh-owned companies ANR Securities, RHC Holding, Ranchem, and Malvinder Singh, as trustee of Bhai Hospital Trust, "hold and control" Prius Real Estate, into which they infused funds through debentures. The book value of debentures held by these four entities in Prius Real Estate amounted to ₹1,429.5 crore. Daiichi also alleged that the Singhs used their jointly-owned entity, Shimal Healthcare, to divert ₹1,407.33 crore through preference shares and debentures.

Daiichi accused the Singhs of operating through a web of companies to shield their assets, stating, "A large sum of money to the tune of several thousand crores has been extended to various group entities. This is a clear act of fraudulent diversion and siphoning of funds." In the Fortis healthcare case, the Singh brothers were accused of diverting ₹472 crore to their personal companies. The brothers have denied all allegations.

In October 2019, Malvinder and Shivinder Singh were arrested by the Economic Offences Wing (EOW) of the Delhi Police for allegedly causing a loss of ₹2,397 crore to Religare Finvest. Other arrests included those of Sunil Godhwani, a Singh family confidant and former chairman and managing director of Religare Enterprises; and Kavi Arora and Anil Saxena, who held important managerial positions in REL and RFL.

> The Singh brothers claimed that a large portion
> of the family's wealth was transferred to their
> spiritual guru, Gurinder Singh Dhillon, head of
> the Radha Soami Satsang Beas.

The Singh brothers claimed that a large portion of the family's wealth was transferred to their spiritual guru, Gurinder Singh Dhillon, head of the Radha Soami Satsang Beas. The charges against the brothers and other top officials included Section 409 (criminal breach of trust by a public servant, banker, merchant, or agent) and Section 420 (cheating) of the Indian Penal Code. "The alleged persons, having absolute control of Religare Enterprises and its subsidiaries, put Religare Finvest in poor financial condition by distributing loans to companies with no financial standing, causing a loss to RFL of ₹2,397 crore," the EOW stated. The complaint was filed by RFL with the Delhi Police in September 2019.

Additionally, a Singapore tribunal ordered the Singhs in 2016 to pay ₹3,500 crore to Daiichi Sankyo after finding that they had concealed critical information during the sale of Ranbaxy. In another investigation, the Reserve Bank of India found ₹1,800 crore was diverted to the Singhs' holding company, and demanded repayment. Lenders seized the shares pledged to them, including those of Fortis and Religare, leading to minority shareholders taking control of Religare. By 2019, Saluja was tasked by the minority shareholders to turn around the company.

While the Singhs were in jail, the Delhi Police received a tip-off from the Enforcement Directorate about extortion from Aditi Singh, wife of Shivinder Singh. An investigation revealed that one Sukesh Chandrasekhar and his associates had extorted ₹200 crore from Aditi, posing as Home Ministry officials, and promising bail for her husband. Chandrasekhar and his wife, Leena Maria Paul, were arrested in September 2022.

Further investigations revealed that Sukesh had given expensive gifts to several film stars, including Jacqueline Fernandez, a Bollywood actor, with the money allegedly taken from Aditi Singh. In December 2023, Fernandez moved the Delhi High Court to dismiss the case against her, claiming the money laundering allegations were false, and that she was also a victim. The ED had accused Fernandez of enjoying the proceeds of the alleged crime.

In June 2023, the Delhi High Court granted bail to Malvinder Singh, while the Saket court granted bail to Shivinder Singh. Both had been arrested in October 2019 for alleged misappropriation of funds from Religare Finvest.

THE SALUJA PLAN

When Saluja took over as the Executive Chairperson of Religare, the company faced significant challenges, particularly with its lending vertical, Religare Finvest

(RFL). The RBI had prohibited RFL from expanding its credit and investment portfolios, except for government securities, and banned it from paying dividends until further notice.

This action followed the meltdown of IL&FS, a Mumbai-based financial services firm, that collapsed under heavy debt. Concerned about the health of other non-banking financial companies, the RBI closely monitored the sector.

Under its new management, RFL focused on collection and recoveries to meet its repayment obligations to Indian banks. Along with its parent company, RFL devised a debt resolution plan with its lenders and regulators, and decided to bring in a strategic investor. Despite making profits, Religare Housing Development Finance Corporation, a subsidiary of RFL, faced the cascading effects of RFL's problems.

Religare Broking (RBL), a wholly-owned subsidiary, also struggled, reporting a loss of ₹21.46 crore in FY 2019-20. The broking firm suffered from a lack of capital and liquidity, which constrained its business volume growth despite having a robust clientele, infrastructure, and technology platform.

As the company incurred losses, its credit rating was downgraded due to financial stress at the group level, restricting access to bank finance and capital. Saluja and the board tackled the challenge head-on, engaging with various stakeholders including investors, lenders, employees, and business partners.

> As the company incurred losses, its credit rating was downgraded due to financial stress at the group level, restricting access to bank finance and capital.

Religare and RFL pursued all regulatory and legal actions, both civil and criminal, to recover funds diverted from the Religare group. The company raised necessary capital directly and through its subsidiaries, to support the growth of its material businesses.

"In fiscal year 2020, the company received primary capital of ₹161.5 crore as warrant conversion money and ₹200 crore from the sale of its 6.4 per cent stake in Care Health Insurance. These funds were used to pay off obligations and invest in subsidiaries. The company also actively pursued legal and recovery cases and settled past disputes, which were bottlenecks to growth," Saluja informed Religare shareholders in her first communication as Executive Chairperson for the fiscal year ending March 2020. She reassured investors that the company would soon return to its growth path.

The stake sale and involvement of new investors significantly contributed to the business and financial well-being of Religare, providing the necessary capital for growth and helping resolve legacy issues and financial stress in its lending business.

The capital raised from investors was used to pay off bank debt and fund subsidiaries, ensuring their solvency and restoring confidence among shareholders.

The capital raised from investors was used to pay off bank debt and fund subsidiaries, ensuring their solvency and restoring confidence among shareholders. This fundraising took place even amid the Covid-19 pandemic, when the country was experiencing lockdowns.

For FY 2020, Religare Enterprises reported a loss of ₹1,037 crore, an improvement compared to the previous year's loss of ₹1,500 crore on a consolidated basis. The company attributed the loss to an additional provision of ₹387 crore against loans and investments by Religare Finvest, and a settlement payment of ₹170 crore to Axis Bank.

In March 2020, the RBI rejected Religare's application to sell a stake in RFL to TCG Advisory Services, a private equity firm. Nevertheless, RFL managed to pay ₹837 crore to its lenders by raising funds from the conversion of warrants issued to several investors. The total payment made to banks was ₹1,517 crore, including ₹876 crore with the State

Bank of India by March 2020. After the fiscal year-end, the company submitted a turnaround plan to its lenders, which included selling a stake to potential investors. Religare also started the process of disassociating from the former promoters, the Singh brothers, by applying to the stock exchanges. In June 2021, Religare raised additional funds from the Burmans and SSG Capital through preferential allotment of shares.

On May 31, 2022, RFL received a communication from its lead lender informing it that the lenders had agreed in principle to consider a one-time settlement (OTS) proposal for RFL. This proposal was approved by the lenders by December 2022, marking a crucial step in the company's turnaround.

As the pandemic subsided, Saluja informed shareholders that the company had become debt-free on a standalone basis by eliminating all outstanding debt.

As the pandemic subsided, Saluja informed shareholders that the company had become debt-free on a standalone basis by eliminating all outstanding debt. "In July 2021, we raised ₹570 crore through a preferential issue from a mix of current shareholders and new investors to fuel growth and expansion. The company invested most of these funds in its subsidiaries to expand and revitalize their operations," Saluja stated.

For FY 2022, Religare Broking reported a revenue of ₹284 crore, a significant improvement from the previous year. The profit after tax for RBL was ₹22.6 crore, more than double the previous year's profit.

"RBL is also registered with SEBI to act as a Registrar to an issue and share transfer agent from April 5, 2022. We infused additional equity of ₹50 crore in RBL in August 2021 to further invest in products, technology, and other areas for achieving accelerated and profitable growth," Saluja added. "The company views the retail broking space as an essential area of growth, and aspires for RBL to reclaim its position as one of the top ten brokers in the country."

The health insurance business—Care Health Insurance— in which REL holds a 65.5 per cent equity stake, registered phenomenal growth. The firm reported a gross written premium of ₹3,947 crore, a 53 per cent increase over the previous year, and a profit before tax of over ₹15 crore.

In the same year, the company succeeded in reclassifying the Singh brothers from promoters to public shareholders, making Religare a "listed entity with no promoters". While stabilizing operations, the company pursued all regulatory and legal actions against the former promoters to recover funds allegedly diverted by the Singh brothers.

Religare officials highlighted notable actions by Saluja, including a strategic shift from selling off all businesses (NBFC, broking, and health insurance) to a full-scale revival, establishing Religare as a diversified financial services brand.

With the board's efforts, RFL was poised for growth, post-removal of the RBI corrective action plan, in place since January 2018. By mid-2023, the company had a positive net worth and adequate capital, and began discussions with potential lenders and investors to restart RFL's business.

Meanwhile, another group firm—Religare Housing Development Finance Corporation—adopted a unique approach to serving underserved, low-income, and informal segments by providing home purchase, construction, and improvement loans with a robust underwriting framework, effectively addressing market gaps.

A significant milestone for the group was the transformation in the health sector.

A significant milestone for the group was the transformation in the health sector. After the 2020 pandemic, the demand for health care products, including hospitals and insurance, rose significantly. Care Health Insurance led the insurance space and received funding from private equity players like Kedaara Capital, which invested ₹567 crore in June 2020 for a 16 per cent stake.

Religare officials noted the management's initiative to embrace technological advancements through industry partnerships, including collaboration with the Nasscom Centre of Excellence. This partnership aims to strengthen REL's business processes and solutions through cutting-edge technology and innovation. Religare also seeks strategic investment opportunities in startups to foster innovation and drive growth in the financial services sector.

Under Saluja's leadership, Religare seeded new businesses synergistic to overall growth. "The recent acquisition of MyInsuranceClub is one such example. Building Religare 2.0 is based on a deep understanding of our distinct businesses across health insurance, lending, and stock broking. We strategically allocate resources to meet the unique needs of each unit," an official said.

Religare enhanced value for stakeholders, including shareholders, employees, and customers, while maintaining high corporate governance standards.

Religare enhanced value for stakeholders, including shareholders, employees, and customers, while maintaining high corporate governance standards. Saluja's commitment to growth enabled the company to navigate its transformation over the past five years. Her leadership helped defend the company from external challenges, and reshape it from within.

This progress was evident in the company's financials for FY 2023. Religare paid the final one-time settlement amount of ₹2,178 crore to lenders in March 2023. RFL also signed an Upside Sharing Agreement with lenders, agreeing to share 70% of the principal and half of the interest on the Fixed Deposit Receipt deposited with Lakshmi Vilas Bank (now DBS), and 60% of recoveries from the Corporate Loan Book, subject to actual recoveries.

Considering the upfront OTS payments and the Upside Sharing Agreement, RFL wrote off advances/loans of ₹1,222 crore and fixed deposits of ₹559 crore to be shared with lenders. It also wrote back the liability towards principal and interest of lenders of ₹388 crore and the provision of ₹1,222 crore, resulting in a net gain of ₹3,289 crore on extinguishment of borrowings under the OTS. As of March 31, 2023, RFL's Capital to Risk (Weighted) Assets Ratio (CRAR) was a positive 48.94%, compared to a negative CRAR of 199.53% the previous year.

After assuming leadership, Saluja focused on capital allocation and governance. In FY 2023, the health insurance business received adequate capital for continued growth.

REL fully subscribed to the rights issue of Care Health Insurance, which reported a gross written premium of ₹5,237.69 crore, a 33% increase over the previous year, and a profit before tax of ₹327.96 crore.

The broking business, infused with additional capital in FY22, turned around and grew at better than market benchmarks. The management supported the broking business in its banking relationships, enhancing funding lines from various lenders. The total revenue of Religare Broking and its subsidiary, Religare Commodities, increased from ₹284.26 crore in FY22, to ₹292 crore in FY23.

The affordable housing finance business managed to grow its loan book despite funding challenges since 2018.

The affordable housing finance business managed to grow its loan book despite funding challenges since 2018. With incremental lending continuing from collections, the housing finance business is poised for higher growth with improved liability profiles following the change of its promoter from RFL to REL.

Religare has not only turned around but is now ready to take off.

IMPROVING FINANCIAL HEALTH

As financial year ending March 2024 came to a close, both the Burmans and Religare's board found themselves at a stalemate. The Burman family's open offer was awaiting SEBI clearance, which required no-objection approvals from the RBI and the IRDAI. This clearance was essential for the Burmans to increase their stake from 21% and above via the open offer.

While awaiting SEBI's verdict, the Religare board was busy planning for the future. They aimed to launch an initial public offering (IPO) for Care Health Insurance, providing an exit for private equity investors. Given the strong valuations for health insurance companies in the stock market, investment bankers expect the company to list with a valuation of ₹15,000 crore, boosting the parent company's plans to become a financial powerhouse.

Rating agencies, which had lost hope in the group companies in 2018, were now supportive of the new management's turnaround strategy. In December 2023, CRISIL Ratings, a rating firm, assigned better ratings to Religare Broking's bank loan facilities of ₹350 crore, acknowledging the company's adequate capitalization, long track record, and effective risk management systems. RBL reported a steady rise in its net worth to ₹230 crore as of September 30, 2023, up from ₹217.71 crore on March 31, 2023, and ₹207.87 crore on March 31, 2022.

CRISIL noted that RBL's gearing remained comfortable at 0.97 times as of September 30, 2023, and projected it to stay within 1-2 times on a steady-state basis. The company's capitalization was also supported by REL's history of equity infusions and inter-corporate credit lines, with a total equity capital of ₹230.8 crore raised from REL since inception. This, along with sustained internal accruals, was expected to support RBL's capital position over the medium term.

With the stock market booming in 2023, the brokering industry experienced significant transformation, led by technology-based discount and online brokers like Zerodha. CRISIL highlighted RBL's efforts to achieve scale-based growth and restore its market position in retail brokerage and allied services, emphasizing the need for a resilient business model to manage competition and grow market share.

Religare Housing Development Finance Corporation, a subsidiary of Religare Finvest, also received a positive rating from CARE Ratings in August 2023, as it raised ₹500 crore in debts. CARE Ratings noted the company's adequate liquidity, with investments in liquid mutual funds and unutilized credit lines from Religare Enterprises. The rating reflected the company's comfortable capitalization with a gearing of 0.25x and successful completion of a one-time settlement (OTS) with Religare Finvest's lenders.

Post-OTS, RFL's standard assets were sufficient to cover its unsecured debt, limiting the need for external funding. However, RFL remained under the RBI's Corrective Action Plan framework, preventing it from making incremental disbursements or investments (except in government securities), a key constraint. Religare Enterprises plans to purchase an 87.5% equity stake in the housing finance firm from RFL, pending regulatory approval.

Despite financial challenges at the parent level, the housing finance company maintained asset quality and collection efficiency.

Despite financial challenges at the parent level, the housing finance company maintained asset quality and collection efficiency. The credit cost to average total assets remained below 0.5% over the past three years, and net non-performing assets (NPA) reduced to 2.7% as of March 31, 2023, from 6% as of March 31, 2021. Since 2017, the company had repaid nearly ₹1,000 crore to lenders through collections, without refinancing. The gearing level decreased to 0.25x as of March 31, 2023, from 1.3x as of March 31, 2021, and the capital adequacy ratio improved to 124.5% from 67.7% during this period. CARE Ratings indicated that RFL's assets were sufficient to cover its remaining unsettled debt, eliminating the need for external support from the Religare group for debt settlement.

With Saluja's turnaround plan reaching its final stage and all companies back in the black, the battle for control of Religare Enterprises has intensified. The parent company's valuation is set to increase with the listing of the health care insurance firm, raising the stakes for both the Burmans and Saluja.

ENTER THE "WHITE KNIGHT": DRAMA AT THE AGM

In December 2024, SEBI approved the Burman family office's open offer for Religare Enterprises; this was formally announced on January 18, 2025. The offer coincided with the company's annual shareholders' meeting on February 7, which included a resolution on the reappointment of Saluja as a director on the board. With a majority of shareholders led by the Burman family turning against Saluja, her fate was sealed.

But a surprise was in store. Just as the open offer was launched on January 22, Digvijay "Danny" Gaekwad, a businessman from Florida, made a counteroffer to buy 55 per cent stake in Religare Enterprises at ₹275 per share, surpassing the Burmans' offer of ₹235 a share. In his communication to SEBI, Gaekwad said his offer represented a 17 per cent premium to the open offer price made by the Burmans, and a 24 per cent premium to the

60-day volume weighted average price of REL's shares calculated with a reference date of September 22, 2023, at ₹221. The SEBI, however, returned the counteroffer, prompting Gaekwad to move the Supreme Court. The Burmans also contested the counteroffer saying that it was not made within 15 days from the date of the public statement given by the Burmans, on October 4, 2023.

In a telephone interview from Florida, Gaekwad—who runs a real estate business in the USA and a coffee plantation in Colombia—stated that the Burmans' offer undervalued the company, and that *his* offer was in the best interests of all shareholders. "Who loses if my counteroffer of ₹275 per share is rejected by SEBI? Is it me or the shareholders?" argued Gaekwad, who entered the takeover battle as a white knight.

Gaekwad, a staunch supporter of the American Republican Party and US President Donald Trump, argued that SEBI should have given him the opportunity to make the counteroffer, as it was in the best interest of all stakeholders, including the management. The offer also gained support from Saluja, who believed that the company's shares should be priced higher due to its remarkable turnaround.

In the Supreme Court, Gaekwad's lawyers argued that the public offer should be based on the higher of two values: the acquisition price as of September 25, 2023, or the market price prevailing at the time of the public offer, on

January 18, 2025. In its order dated February 7, 2025, the Supreme Court said that SEBI's primary concern should be the rights and interests of public investors, and hence decided to give an opportunity to Gaekwad to make an offer.

With the tendering period for shares closing the same day, the Court extended the deadline to February 12, 2025, requiring Gaekwad to deposit ₹600 crore with the authorities to fund his counteroffer. The Supreme Court's ruling placed Gaekwad in a tight spot, as he had four days to either deposit the funds for his counteroffer, or bow out of the race.

While the Supreme Court arguments were going on, another drama was playing out in the online shareholders' meeting of Religare. Saluja—who chaired the meeting—made an emotional plea to the shareholders to support her while voting. At the AGM, which was to decide her fate, Saluja reiterated that the financial year ending March 2024 was a year of robust performance for REL and its subsidiaries. "Our management team is relentlessly working to revitalize and expand operations while maintaining the highest standards of corporate governance, and being a responsible corporate citizen. We are focused on continuing our operational growth momentum and creating value for our stakeholder ecosystem," she said, as she reiterated that she was not liable to retire by rotation.

Saluja said that Religare's health insurance arm—Care Health Insurance—was the second largest standalone health insurer, and was one of the fastest-growing in the industry. "When CHIL surpassed the significant ₹7,000 crore mark in gross written premium—a 34% growth—it not only marked a financial milestone, but also demonstrated the trust of millions of customers who turned to us for security in uncertain times. Care Health now operates 262 branches and has a network of over 24,820 hospitals and healthcare centres," Saluja informed the shareholders.

"Our securities broking arm, Religare Broking, achieved 28% growth despite stiff competition. This reflects not only strong financial results but also our agility and focus on technological advancements to meet evolving customer needs. I'm pleased to report that our e-governance business continues to expand exponentially, with over 43,800 touch points across the country. Religare Broking remains focused on integrating artificial intelligence and new digital technologies to offer cutting-edge services," she said.

About the group's NBFC arm—Religare Finance— Saluja recapped that after completing the full and final settlement of its outstanding debts in March 2023, it had taken multiple steps to revive the business. "These measures include improvements in the asset and liability management position, capital to risk (weighted) ratio, and the removal of the fraud tag from certain banks. With these positive developments, management is confident that the cap will be removed and the lending business will resume shortly. With no debt liabilities, the subsidiary is poised to restart operations as soon as the cap is lifted, and all necessary teams and systems are in place to roll out the business in the near term," she said.

Religare Housing Development Finance Corporation Limited (RHDFCL), the housing finance arm, was providing affordable housing finance to underserved customers employed in the formal sector. "It operates in ten states, serving both urban and semi-urban areas. RHDFCL's growth plans align with the Government of India's Housing for All initiative, and we are committed to meeting our customers' housing finance needs through 29 branches across the country. RHDFCL has established strategic co-lending partnerships with reputable housing finance companies and an NBFC, further strengthening its position in the market," Saluja said, and promised to transform Religare into a 360-degree financial services conglomerate. "We are poised to seize incremental opportunities in every segment we operate in. Our management team is tirelessly working to transform Religare, combining best business practices with unmatched ethics to maximize stakeholder and shareholder value."

Since 2018, Religare has undergone a remarkable transformation—from a company facing legacy challenges to a thriving financial services entity. "This is a testament to the management's unwavering commitment to excellence. We have effectively eliminated all outstanding debts and are now a debt-free entity, with profitable operations across all business segments—delivering significant value to shareholders," Saluja said in her remarks.

"The strategic vision and efforts of the management have established Religare as a leading player in the financial services sector. While this has created substantial value for stakeholders, it has also sparked renewed interest in the market, positioning the company as one of the most attractive acquisition targets in the sector," she stated.

Saluja recalled that in September 2023, the open offer was launched by the Burman Group. Following SEBI guidelines, the Committee of Independent Directors (CID) was formed to evaluate the offer. "One of the first things that caught their attention was that the prevailing market price was around ₹280 a share, while the open offer was set at ₹235. This price disparity raised concerns," she said.

Saluja mentioned that the same shareholders, including the Burmans, had previously appreciated the board and the management for successfully turning the company around and creating value. "In February 2018, when the former promoters left, the company was in disarray, with its future uncertain. There was real concern that the company might be forced into NCLT or liquidated. However, the management stayed committed, working tirelessly to stabilize and revive the company. The turnaround was challenging, but no one anticipated the company would achieve the success it has today. The management stayed on, despite numerous legal cases and external threats," Saluja said about the Enforcement Directorate notices on the ESOPs (employee stock options) received by her. "Thanks to their perseverance and strong governance, the company began to attract investors,"

She continued, "Year after year, our performance improved—from a share price of ₹17 (at the time of the crisis) to much higher levels. This was the result of tireless work and the shared goal of becoming a beacon of change. The company was on the brink of collapse, and at that time, the board made it clear that they were not there to sell the company or act as a stopgap. The goal was to ensure the company survived, thrived, and became adequately funded," she said. She then recalled how during the last 18 months, the management faced harassment from agencies, but they continued to fight for justice for the company. "The company navigated a complex maze of legal battles and statutory hurdles, yet we managed to come out strong, settling everything with SEBI, and launching a restructuring plan."

Saluja said the management worked tirelessly to restore the trust of the lenders by repaying them. "Over ₹9,500 crore was repaid through a one-time settlement (OTS), which was completed ahead of schedule," she recalled.

The company's recovery was extraordinary, especially considering the turbulent times in India's financial sector, with other major firms like IL&FS, Reliance Capital, DHFL, and Yes Bank also facing difficulties. "Through sincerity and determination, the management earned the trust of the lenders. After settling the fraud tag, the company began to move forward. Care Health Insurance gained strength, and other segments like Religare Broking and the NBFC business also showed positive results." Saluja reiterated that throughout all these challenges, the management team remained unchanged for six years, and the shareholders continued to support the company. "During tough times, the management even put their own money into the business to keep things afloat. This collaboration between the management, the board, and the shareholders created an environment of trust and collective commitment," she said.

The committee of independent directors had thoroughly evaluated the open offer, and despite concerns regarding the offer price, they acted with fiduciary responsibility to protect shareholders' interests. "They raised valid points to the appropriate authorities, but were unfortunately met with resistance. This triggered a prolonged battle between the management and the acquirer companies, and the years of turnaround efforts became clouded in a contentious situation," she said.

The decisions made in the past were questioned, undermining the work that had been done to rebuild the company. The core issue was the perceived inadequacy of the open offer price, but the real question was whether the company would be allowed to continue its growth trajectory or forced to clean up past mistakes, she summed up.

Despite her eloquent plea, 97 per cent of the shareholders voted against Saluja. By February 13, Danny Gaekwad, who feared litigation risk in India, failed to deposit the money required of him and his counteroffer collapsed. Saluja, who had steered Religare through its most turbulent times, was ousted from the board.

The Burmans, having emerged victorious in the takeover battle, promised to lead the company to new heights. Will the Burmans achieve their objective without Saluja? That's the billion dollar question.

CITATION

Raghavan, Prabha. "Malvinder and Shivinder Singh and the 'missing' funds of a billion-dollar empire." The Indian Express, 15 Apr. 2019, www.indianexpress.com/article/ business/companies/daiichi-sankyo-case-fortis-healhcare- supreme-court-ranbaxy-arbitral-award-malvinder- shivinder-singh-5675625/

LIST OF ABBREVIATIONS IN THE BOOK

ARC: Asset Reconstruction Company

BIFR: Board for Industrial and Financial Reconstruction

BPO: Business Process Outsourcing

BSE: Bombay Stock Exchange

CDR: Corporate Debt Restructuring

CRAR: Capital to Risk (Weighted) Assets Ratio

DRI: Direct reduced iron

EBITDA: Earnings before interest, tax, depreciation, and amortization

EOW: Economic Offences Wing

EPC: Engineering, procurement, and construction

ERP: Enterprise Resource Planning

ESOP: Employee Stock Ownership Plan

FY: Fiscal Year

GST: Goods and Services Tax

GW: Gigawatt

IBBI: Insolvency and Bankruptcy Board of India

IBC: Insolvency and Bankruptcy Code, 2016

IIM: Indian Institute of Management

IIT: Indian Institute of Technology

IMEC: India-Middle East-Europe Economic Corridor

ISB: Indian School of Business

JVSL: Jindal Vijayanagar Steel Limited

L&T: Larsen and Toubro

LIC: Life Insurance Corporation

LVB: Lakshmi Vilas Bank

M&A: Mergers and acquisitions

MIS: Management Information Systems

MPPL: Maini Precision Products Limited

MTPA: Million tonnes per annum

MW: Megawatt

NCLAT: National Company Law Appellate Tribunal

NCLT: National Company Law Tribunal

NINL: Neelachal Ispat Nigam Limited

NPA: Non-Performing Asset

NWC: Net working capital

OCD: Optionally Convertible Debentures

OTS: One-Time Settlement

PPP: Public-private partnership

RBI: Reserve Bank of India

RBL: Religare Broking Limited

RCCL: Raymond Consumer Care Limited

REL: Religare Enterprises Limited

RERA: Real Estate (Regulation and Development) Act, 2016

RFL: Religare Finvest Ltd

RIL: Reliance Industries Limited

RPAL: Ring Plus Aqua Limited

SAP: Systems, Applications, and Products

SC: Supreme Court

SDR: Strategic Debt Restructuring (scheme)

SEBI: Securities and Exchange Board of India

SISCOL: Southern Iron and Steel Company

SPV: Special Purpose Vehicle

TQM: Total Quality Management

WTO: World Trade Organization

ABOUT THE AUTHORS

Pragya Chatterjee, a graduate of the University of Oklahoma, started her career as an intern with the Tata Trusts and Zensar Technologies. She has contributed her expertise to several institutions such as the Carl Albert Congressional Research and Studies Center and other entities worldwide. Pragya has also served as a dedicated research assistant for the University of Oklahoma, showcasing her passion for academic exploration, a multifaceted approach to making an impact, and commitment to a global perspective.

Dev Chatterjee is an alumnus of the University of California, Berkeley, and the University of Mumbai. Dev has worked with *Business Standard*, *The Indian Express*, *The Economic Times* and *ET Now* as a senior journalist.